BRIGHT NOTES

OTHELLO
BY
WILLIAM
SHAKESPEARE

Intelligent Education

INFLUENCE PUBLISHERS

Nashville, Tennessee

BRIGHT NOTES: Othello

www.BrightNotes.com

No part of this publication may be used or reproduced in any manner whatsoever without written permission, except in the case of brief quotations in critical articles and reviews. For permissions, contact Influence Publishers http://www.influencepublishers.com.

ISBN: 978-1-645425-76-2 (Paperback)
ISBN: 978-1-645425-77-9 (eBook)

Published in accordance with the U.S. Copyright Office Orphan Works and Mass Digitization report of the register of copyrights, June 2015.

Originally published by Monarch Press.
William Joseph Grace, 1964
2020 Edition published by Influence Publishers.

Interior design by Lapiz Digital Services. Cover Design by Thinkpen Designs.

Printed in the United States of America.

Library of Congress Cataloging-in-Publication Data forthcoming.
Names: Intelligent Education
Title: BRIGHT NOTES: Othello
Subject: STU004000 STUDY AIDS / Book Notes

CONTENTS

1)   Introduction to William Shakespeare   1

2)   Introduction to Othello   12

3)   Textual Analysis   18
       Act 1: Scenes 1 and 2   18
       Act 1: Scene 3   33
       Act 2   50
       Act 3   72
       Act 4   103
       Act 5   116

4)   Character Analyses   127

5)   Critical Commentary   159

6)   Essay Questions and Answers   176

7)   Bibliography   192

INTRODUCTION TO WILLIAM SHAKESPEARE

. . . .

FACTS VERSUS SPECULATION

Anyone who wishes to know where documented truth ends and where speculation begins in Shakespearean scholarship and criticism first needs to know the facts of Shakespeare's life. A medley of life records suggest, by their lack of inwardness, how little is known of Shakespeare's ideology, his beliefs and opinions.

William Shakespeare was baptized on April 26, 1564, as "Gulielmus filius Johannes Shakspere"; the evidence is the parish register of Holy Trinity Church, Stratford, England.

HUSBAND AND FATHER

On November 28, 1582, the Bishop of Worcester issued a license to William Shakespeare and "Anne Hathwey of Stratford" to solemnize a marriage upon one asking of the banns providing that there were no legal impediments. Three askings of the banns were (and are) usual in the Church of England.

On May 26, 1583, the records of the parish church in Stratford note the baptism of Susanna, daughter to William Shakespeare. The inference is clear, then, that Anne Hathaway Shakespeare was with child at the time of her wedding.

On February 2, 1585, the records of the parish church in Stratford note the baptisms of "Hamnet & Judeth, sonne and daughter to William Shakspere."

SHAKESPEARE INSULTED

On September 20, 1592, Robert Greene's A Groats-worth of witte, bought with a million of Repentance was entered in the Stationers' Register. In this work Shakespeare was publicly insulted as "an upstart Crow, beautified with our ["gentlemen" playwrights usually identified as Marlowe, Nashe, and Lodge] feathers, that with Tygers hart wrapt in a Players hyde [a **parody** of a Shakespearean line in II *Henry VI*] supposes he is as well able to bombast out a **blank verse** as the best of you: and being an absolute Iohannes fac totum, is in his own conceit the only Shake-scene in a country." This statement asperses not only Shakespeare's art but intimates his base, i.e., non-gentle, birth. A "John factotum" is a servant or a man of all work.

On April 18, 1593, Shakespeare's long erotic poem *Venus and Adonis* was entered for publication. It was printed under the author's name and was dedicated to the nineteen-year-old Henry Wriothesley, Earl of Southampton.

On May 9, 1594, another long erotic poem, *The Rape of Lucrece*, was entered for publication. It also was printed under Shakespeare's name and was dedicated to the Earl of Southampton.

On December 26 and 27, 1594, payment was made to Shakespeare and others for performances at court by the Lord Chamberlain's servants.

For August 11, 1596, the parish register of Holy Trinity Church records the burial of "Hamnet filius William Shakspere."

FROM "VILLEIN" TO "GENTLEMAN"

On October 20, 1596, John Shakespeare, the poet's father, was made a "gentleman" by being granted the privilege of bearing a coat of arms. Thus, William Shakespeare on this day also became a "gentleman." Shakespeare's mother, Mary Arden Shakespeare, was "gentle" by birth. The poet was a product of a cross-class marriage. Both the father and the son were technically "villeins" or "villains" until this day.

On May 24, 1597, William Shakespeare purchased New Place, a large house in the center of Stratford.

CITED AS "BEST"

In 1598 Francis Meres's *Palladis Tamia* listed Shakespeare more frequently than any other English author. Shakespeare was cited as one of eight by whom "the English tongue is mightily enriched, and gorgeouslie invested in rare ornaments and resplendent abiliments"; as one of six who had raised monumentum aere perennius [a monument more lasting than brass]; as one of five who excelled in lyric poetry; as one of thirteen "best for Tragedie," and as one of seventeen who were "best for Comedy."

On September 20, 1598, Shakespeare is said on the authority of Ben Jonson (in his collection of plays, 1616) to have been an actor in Jonson's *Every Man in His Humour.*

On September 8, 1601, the parish register of Holy Trinity in Stratford records the burial of "Mr. Johannes Shakespeare," the poet's father.

BECOMES A "KING'S MAN"

In 1603 Shakespeare was named among others, the Lord Chamberlain's players, as licensed by James I (Queen Elizabeth having died) to become the King's Men.

In 1603 a garbled and pirated *Hamlet* (now known as *Q1*) was printed with Shakespeare's name on the title page.

In March 1604, King James gave Shakespeare, as one of the Grooms of the Chamber (by virtue of being one of the King's Men), four yards of red cloth for a livery, this being in connection with a royal progress through the City of London.

In 1604 (probably) there appeared a second version of *Hamlet* (now known as *Q2*), enlarged and corrected, with Shakespeare's name on the title page.

On June 5, 1607, the parish register at Stratford records the marriage of "M. John Hall gentleman & Susanna Shaxspere," the poet's elder daughter. John Hall was a doctor of medicine.

BECOMES A GRANDFATHER

On February 21, 1608, the parish register at Holy Trinity, Stratford, records the baptism of Elizabeth Hall, Shakespeare's first grandchild.

On September 9, 1608, the parish register at Holy Trinity, Stratford, records the burial of Mary Shakespeare, the poet's mother.

On May 20, 1609, "Shakespeares Sonnets. Never before Imprinted" was entered for publication.

On February 10, 1616, the marriage of Judith, Shakespeare's younger daughter, is recorded in the parish register of Holy Trinity, Stratford.

On March 25, 1616, Shakespeare made his will. It is extant.

On April 23, 1616, Shakespeare died. The monument in the Stratford church is authority for the date.

BURIED IN STRATFORD CHURCH

On April 25, 1616, Shakespeare was buried in Holy Trinity Church, Stratford. Evidence of this date is found in the church register. A stone laid over his grave bears the inscription:

Good Frend for Jesus Sake Forbeare, To Digg The Dust Encloased Heare! Blest Be Ye Man Yt Spares Thes Stones, And Curst Be He Yt Moves My Bones.

DEMAND FOR MORE INFORMATION

These are the life records of Shakespeare. Biographers, intent on book length or even short accounts of the life of the poet, of necessity flesh out these (and other) not very revealing notices from 1564-1616, Shakespeare's life span with ancillary matter such as the status of Elizabethan actors, details of the Elizabethan theaters, and life under Elizabeth I and James I. Information about Shakespeare's artistic life-for example, his alteration of his sources-is much more abundant than truthful insights into his personal life, including his beliefs. There is, of course, great demand for colorful stories about Shakespeare, and there is intense pressure on biographers to depict the poet as a paragon of wisdom.

ANECDOTES-TRUE OR UNTRUE?

Biographers of Shakespeare may include stories about Shakespeare that have been circulating since at least the seventeenth century; no one knows whether or not these stories are true. One declares that Shakespeare was an apprentice to a butcher, that he ran away from his master, and was received by actors in London. Another story holds that Shakespeare was, in his youth, a schoolmaster somewhere in the country. Another story has Shakespeare fleeing from his native town to escape the clutches of Sir Thomas Lucy who had often had him whipped and sometimes imprisoned for poaching deer. Yet another story represents the youthful Shakespeare as holding horses and taking care of them while their owners attended the theater. And there are other stories.

Scholarly and certainly lay expectations oblige Shakespearean biographers often to resort to speculation. This may be very well if biographers use such words as conjecture, presumably, seems, and almost certainly. I quote an example of this kind of hedged thought and language from Hazelton Spencer's *The Art and Life of William Shakespeare* (1940); "Of politics Shakespeare seems to have steered clear... but at least by implication Shakespeare reportedly endorses the strong-monarchy policy of the Tudors and Stuarts." Or one may say, as I do in my book *Blood Will Tell in Shakespeare's Plays* (1984): "Shakespeare particularly faults his numerous villeins for lacking the classical virtue of courage (they are cowards) and for deficiencies in reasoning ability (they are 'fools'), and in speech (they commit malapropisms), for lack of charity, for ambition, for unsightly faces and poor physiques, for their smell, and for their harboring lice." This remark is not necessarily biographical or reflective of Shakespeare's personal beliefs; it refers to Shakespeare's art in that it makes general assertions about the base - those who lacked coats of arms-as they appear in the poet's thirty-seven plays. The remark's truth or lack of truth may be tested by examination of Shakespeare's writings.

WHO WROTE SHAKESPEARE'S PLAYS?

The less reputable biographers of Shakespeare, including some of weighty names, state assumptions as if they were facts concerning the poet's beliefs. Perhaps the most egregious are those who cannot conceive that the Shakespearean plays were written by a person not a graduate of Oxford or Cambridge and destitute of the insights permitted by foreign travel and by life at court. Those of this persuasion insist that the seventeenth Earl of Oxford, Edward de Vere (whose descendant Charles Vere recently spoke up for the Earl's authorship of the Shakespearean plays), or Sir Francis Bacon, or someone else wrote the Shakespearean plays. It is also argued that the stigma of publication would besmirch the honor of an Elizabethan gentleman who published under his own name (unless he could pretend to correct a pirated printing of his writings).

BEN JONSON KNEW HIM WELL

Suffice it here to say that the thought of anyone writing the plays and giving them to the world in the name of Shakespeare would have astonished Ben Jonson, a friend of the poet, who literally praised Shakespeare to the skies for his comedies and tragedies in the fine poem "To the Memory of My Beloved Master the Author, Mr. William Shakespeare, and What He Hath Left Us" (printed in the *First Folio*, 1623). Much more commonplace and therefore much more obtrusive upon the minds of Shakespeare students are those many scholars who are capable of writing, for example, that Shakespeare put more of himself into *Hamlet* than any of his other characters or that the poet had no rigid system of religion or morality. Even George Lyman Kittredge, the greatest American Shakespearean, wrote, "Hamlet's advice to the players has always been understood - and rightly - to embody Shakespeare's own views on the art of acting."

In point of fact, we know nothing of Shakespeare's beliefs or opinions except such obvious inferences as that he must have thought New Place, Stratford, worth buying because he bought it. Even Homer, a very self-effacing poet, differs in this matter from Shakespeare. Twice in the *Iliad* he speaks in his own voice (distinguished from the dialogue of his characters) about certain evil deeds of Achilles. Shakespeare left no letters, no diary, and no prefaces (not counting conventionally obsequious dedications); no Elizabethan Boswell tagged Shakespeare around London and the provinces to record his conversation and thus to reveal his mind. In his plays Shakespeare employed no rainsonneur, or authorial mouthpiece, as some other dramatists have done: contrary to many scholarly assertions, it cannot be proved that Prospero, in *The Tempest* in the speech ending "I'll drown my book" (Act V), and Ulysses, in *Troilus and Cressida* in the long speech on "degree" (Act II), speak Shakespeare's own sentiments. All characters in all Shakespearean plays speak for themselves. Whether they speak also for Shakespeare cannot be proved because documents outside the plays cannot be produced.

As for the sonnets, they have long been the happy hunting ground of biographical crackpots who lack outside documents, who do not recognize that Shakespeare may have been using a persona, and who seem not to know that in Shakespeare's time good **sonnets** were supposed to read like confessions.

Some critics even go to the length of professing to hear Shakespeare speaking in the speech of a character and uttering his private beliefs. An example may be found in A. L. Rowse's *What Shakespeare Read and Thought* (1981): "Nor is it so difficult to know what Shakespeare thought or felt. A writer, Logan Pearsall Smith, had the perception to see that a personal tone of voice enters when Shakespeare is telling you what he thinks, sometimes almost a raised voice; it is more obvious again when he urges the same point over and over."

BUT THERE'S NO PROOF!

Rowse, deeply enamoured of his ability to hear Shakespeare's own thoughts in the speeches of characters speaking in character, published a volume entitled Shakespeare's *Self-Portrait, Passages from His Work* (1984). One critic might hear Shakespeare voicing his own thoughts in a speech in Hamlet; another might hear the author in *Macbeth*. Shakespearean writings can become a vast whispering gallery where Shakespeare himself is heard hic et ubique (here and everywhere), without an atom of documentary proof.

"BETTER SO"

Closer to truth is Matthew Arnold's poem on Shakespeare:

Others abide our question. Thou art free. We ask and ask - thou smilest and art still, Out-topping knowledge. For the loftiest hill, Who to the stars uncrowns his majesty, Planting his steadfast footsteps in the sea, Making the heaven of heavens his dwelling Spares but the cloudy border of his base To the foiled searching of mortality; And thou, who didst the stars and sunbeams know, Self-schooled, self-scanned, self-honored, self-secure, Didst tread the earth unguessed at. - Better so. . . .

Here Arnold has Dichtung und Wahrheit - both poetry and truth - with at least two abatements: he exaggerates Shakespeare's wisdom - the poet, after all, is not God; and Arnold fails to acknowledge that Shakespeare's genius was variously recognized in his own time. Jonson, for example, recorded that the "players [actors of the poet's time] have often mentioned it as an honor to Shakespeare, that in his writing (whatsoever he penned) he never blotted a line" (*Timber*), and of course there is praise of Shakespeare, some of it quoted above, in Meres's *Palladis Tamia* (1598).

THE BEST APPROACH

Hippocrates' first apothegm states, "Art is long, but life is short." Even Solomon complained of too many books. One must be, certainly in our time, very selective. Shakespeare's ipsissima verba (his very words) should of course be studied, and some of them memorized. Then, if one has time, the golden insights of criticism from the eighteenth century to the present should be perused. (The problem is to find them all in one book!) And the vast repetitiousness, the jejune stating of the obvious, and the rampant subjectivity of much Shakespearean criticism should be shunned.

Then, if time serves, the primary sources of Shakespeare's era should be studied because the plays were not impervious to colorings imparted by the historical matrix. Finally, if the exigencies of life permit, biographers of Shakespeare who distinguish between fact and guesswork, such as Marchette Chute (Shakespeare of London), should be consulted. The happiest situation, pointed to by Jesus in Milton's *Paradise Regained*, is to bring judgment informed by knowledge to whatever one reads.

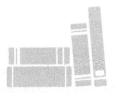

INTRODUCTION TO OTHELLO

Othello was first acted at court on November 1, 1604, and it is generally supposed that the play was written earlier in the same year. **Allusions** in the play to Holland's translation of *Pliny* (1601) and a supposed **allusion** to Dekker and Middleton's play, *The Honest Whore* (1604), set the date at 1604 with more than a fair degree of accuracy.

During the sixteen years which preceded its publication in the First Quarto of 1622, the play was acted "diverse times" at the Globe and Blackfriars theaters in London, where Shakespeare's company, "his Majesties Servants," held their performances. Both the Quarto and Folio editions appear-in 1622, and a second Quarto appeared in 1630 and was reprinted in 1655, all suggesting the considerable interest the public had in *Othello*.

SOURCE

The seventh novella of the third decade of the Hecatommithi by Giovanni Battista Giraldi Cinthio provided the plot for Shakespeare's *Othello*. (The Italian story book, first printed in Venice in 1563, was a frequent source for English stories and plays, and it is entirely possible that Shakespeare learned the tale of the Moor from some other book.)

Like many of his contemporaries, Shakespeare took the plots of his plays from stories in the chronicles of England, from French and Italian tales, from the classical writers, and from other playwrights. But in every case, he altered the original story so brilliantly as to make it his own forever. In Cinthio's tale, the Moor (who has no other name), is highly regarded as a military leader. He is appointed by the lords of Venice to lead an expedition to Cyprus. As in Shakespeare's version, the Moor has married a Venetian lady named Disdemona (sic), who had admired his virtu (manliness, valor). Cinthio's Moor does not relate his adventures to Desdemona, nor does her family object to their marriage. The ensign or alfiere (who becomes Iago in Shakespeare's version) has fallen in love with the Moor's lady and is, indeed, jealous of the captain or capo di squadra (Shakespeare's Cassio). His jealousy is not aroused because the captain has been preferred in appointment, but because the ensign believes that Desdemona's disdain for him is the result of her affection for the captain.

The ensign's love turns to hatred, and he plots revenge against Desdemona. Meanwhile, the captain is dishonored for assaulting a soldier and creating a disturbance while on guard duty. Desdemona, as in Shakespeare's play, takes up his suit with the Moor. The ensign feeds doubt into the Moor's mind about Desdemona's virtue; he claims the captain has boasted of their affair, and he plants her handkerchief (stolen by his own child whom Desdemona has been caressing) in the captain's quarters. The Moor agrees that his wife must be killed and, on the ensign's advice, consents to have him beat her with a sand-filled stocking and pull the weakened ceiling down on her head to conceal the crime.

The ensign beats Desdemona in the Moor's sight. But as soon as the murder is completed the Moor goes mad with grief.

He and the ensign quarrel bitterly, and the Moor deprives the ensign of his office. The ensign contrives to have the Moor recalled to Venice, where he accuses him of murder for the death of Desdemona. Tortured by the authorities, the Moor refuses to confess and is exiled for life. Subsequently, he is killed by Desdemona's kinsmen. The ensign goes free, but later dies under torture in connection with another crime, for he is a thoroughgoing villain, as is Iago. After his death, his wife reveals the true nature of the events concerning the Moor and Desdemona. At no point in Cinthio's story does the Moor become aware of his wife's innocence, nor is this subtlety of characterization necessary in Cinthio's tale, which relied for its interest on the plot alone.

In Shakespeare's adaptation, Othello gains a name, stature, and dignity. He himself undertakes his wife's murder and does not stand idly by while another man saves his honor or works his revenge. In fact, Shakespeare's Moor is anxious to do justice, not take revenge. The handkerchief borrowed from Cinthio's version is given added romance as a magic heirloom, and provides an occasion for *Othello* to demonstrate the power which his wondrous tales of adventure have had on Desdemona. The core of Shakespeare's story - the Moor's inner conflict between his love for Desdemona and the evil suggestion of the ensign-was already present in Cinthio's version. Cinthio also provided numerous vivid portraits of the Moor's distress under the ensign's persistent prodding. But Shakespease rearranges Cinthio's material and makes many new addition in order to develop the characterizations and supply motivations. Because Shakespeare conceives of an ensign too villainous to be the courtly or adulterous suitor of Desdemona, he introduces Roderigo, whom he makes the persistent courtier, foolish, corrupt, but not evil, in the Iago sense, and whom he uses as a foil and accomplice to Iago. In effect, Shakespeare splits

Cinthio's ensign in two; then he makes the two characters work hand in hand to affect their immoral and evil designs. Roderigo is especially useful as a screen upon which Iago can project his negative values, for Iago's values must be examined so that the audience can become convinced, emotionally at least, that under special circumstances, Iago can dominate or "sway" the noble Moor. In addition, Roderigo makes an effective listener like Iago; functioning somewhat like a Greek chorus, he comments on the events of the play.

BRIEF SUMMARY OF OTHELLO

At the opening of the play, Iago and Roderigo are engaged in a heated discussion. From them we learn that Othello, a Moor in the service of the Duke of Venice, has just eloped with Desdemona, a Venetian lady, who has refused Roderigo's offer of marriage. We learn also that Iago hates his general, Othello, and despises a young Florentine captain named Cassie, who has been preferred in an appointment as Othello's lieutenant (his second in command). Iago admits that he continues to follow Othello only to serve his own purposes. He advises Roderigo to warn Brabantio (a Venetian senator, father of Desdemona) of his daughter's elopement. Brabantio complains to the Duke, charging that Othello has enchanted his daughter. But the Duke consents to the unusual marriage, partly because Desdemona asks him to, and partly because he has urgent need of Othello's military service against the Turks in Cyprus. It is arranged under Iago's care. Iago advises Roderigo to sell his estate and join the expedition if he wishes to pursue his courtship of Desdemona.

Iago and Desdemona arrive on Cyprus, where they are courteously greeted by Cassie, Othello's faithful lieutenant. Cassie's courtly manner suggests a plan to Iago by which he can discredit the Moor's lieutenant and wife and work a double revenge against Othello, whom he claims to suspect of having seduced his own wife, Emilia. In addition, he could pretend to be serving Roderigo's love-suit and continue to bilk him of money. Othello now arrives on Cyprus. The Turks, meanwhile, having been drowned during a tempest at sea. He proclaims a general feast to celebrate the victory and his belated honeymoon. Iago contrives to get Cassio drunk, sets Roderigo upon him, and involves the lieutenant in such a "barbarous brawl" that Othello discharges Cassio at once. Next, Iago advises Cassio to enlist Desdemona in his suit for reinstatement. He orders his wife, Emilia, lady-in-waiting to Desdemona, to arrange an interview.

At the interview, Desdemona, promises to serve Cassio's cause. She is so persistent in doing so that the seeds of jealousy, which Iago has planted in the Moor's mind, begin to grow. By the end of the third act, Othello thinks of his wife as a "fair devil" and has appointed Iago his new lieutenant in place of Cassio.

Othello's suspicions are confirmed when he sees Cassio holding a handkerchief, distinguished by its embroidery as the one Othello had given his wife before their marriage. Enraged, Othello strikes Desdemona in front of her kinsman, Lodovico, who has just arrived with messages from Venice. Although Iago's plotting is making rapid progress, Roderigo is still impatient for Desdemona's favors, which Iago has promised to secure for him. At Iago's suggestion, Roderigo agrees to kill his alleged rival, Cassio. Cassio wounds Roderigo, but Iago intervenes in the dark, wounds Cassio, and finishes off Roderigo before he is interrupted.

Now maddened by jealousy, Othello smothers Desdemona in her bed. Emilia arrives in time to hear the faithful Desdemona exonerate her own husband of her murder, but she is too late to save the innocent wife. Emilia learns that Othello has murdered his wife. When she hears of Iago's accusations against Desdemona, she surmises the truth. Emilia cries for help, and when Montano, Gratiano, and Iago respond to her cries, she implicates her husband in the murderous plot. Iago stabs Emilia and flees; Othello is apprehended, and Emilia lies down to die. In the final action of the play, Iago is captured but refuses to speak and utters no other words in the play. Othello wounds Iago and then stabs himself. The injured Cassio is appointed governor of Cyprus, and "the censure of this hellish villain," Iago, is left to his charge.

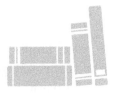

OTHELLO

ACT 1: SCENES 1 AND 2

....

| CHARACTERS

Duke Of Venice. Brabantio, a Venetian senator, father of Desdemona. Gratiano, a brother of Brabantio. Lodovico, a kinsman of Brabantio. Othello, The Moor, a general in the service of Venice. Cassio, lieutenant to Othello, later governor of Cyprus. Iago, ancient (ensign) to Othello, a "villain." Roderigo, a Venetian, the rejected but persistent suitor of Desdemona, and a "gull'd gentleman." Montano, a distinguished citizen of Cyprus. Clown, servant to Othello. Desdemona, a daughter of Brabantio, wife of Othello. Emilia, wife of Iago, lady-in-waiting to Desdemona. Bianca, a courtesan, mistress of Cassio. Sailor, Messengers, Herald, Officers, Gentlemen, Musicians, Attendants.

ACT I: SCENE 1

The scene opens on a street in Venice. It is night. Roderigo and Iago are engaged in a heated discussion over the latter's failure to perform the services he has been paid for, that is, to keep Roderigo informed of Desdemona's affections. Her elopement with Othello the Moor has just come to Roderigo's attention.

Comment

In his list of actors, Shakespeare describes Roderigo as "a gull'd gentleman." A "gull" is the Elizabethan slang for "dupe," equivalent to the American "sucker." Roderigo is Iago's "gull" because he has paid Iago to win Desdemona's love for him, presumably after he has failed to win it himself, while Iago has no intentions of fulfilling his part of the bargain.

Roderigo implies that Iago has abetted the elopement and does not really hate the Moor as he had said. Iago protests. His hatred for the Moor is a very real one, especially since the general has refused to appoint him lieutenant, despite the humble suits made in his behalf by three great men of the city. Iago complains of Othello's pride and "bombast circumstance" and is angered by the appointment, in his stead, of Michael Cassio, an educated military theoretician of Florence, who has had no practical experience in war. Iago himself has shown his courage fighting with the Moor at Rhodes, at Cyprus, against Christians and heathens, but the ungrateful Moor has made Cassio lieutenant, while Iago remains "his Moorship's ancient."

Comment

Roughly, the hierarchy of the Venetian army ran as follows: Othello, full general and supreme commander; Cassio, lieutenant-general and Othello's designated successor; Iago, third in the chain of command, roughly chief-of-staff.

It may be supposed that Iago's hatred of the Moor is a real one. Clearly, he has had a great deal of military experience and is qualified for the post, for later when Cassio is disgraced, Iago is made lieutenant. His quarrel with Cassio's education or "bookishness" reflects the age-old conflict between thinkers and doers. The fact that Cassio is a Florentine probably adds to Iago's anger.

Iago has received payment from Roderigo to press his lovesuit with Desdemona. Presumably, the money was then spent to pay the "three great ones of the city" who lobbied for Iago's appointment as lieutenant. These petitioners seem to have explained their failure to accomplish their mission by attributing to Othello evasive tactics, that is, "bombast circumstance" (roundabout or ceremonious talk). Othello is a proud man, indeed, but he has an open and trusting nature and is not given to evasions in the beginning of the play. This disparagement of his character, therefore, may be attributed to the failure of the "great ones' or to Iago's hatred.

Notice that Iago and Roderigo find themselves in similar circumstances. Iago has been rejected by the Moor; Roderigo by the Moor's wife, Desdemona. The similarity of situation can be traced to the original story of the Moor and "Desdemona" told by Cinthio in the Hecatommithi, where the roles of rejected lover and ensign to the Moor were played by a single character.

At Iago's outburst of grievances, Roderigo expresses surprise that the ancient continues to follow the general whom he hates so much. Iago assures his companion: "I follow him to serve my turn upon him." In following the Moor, Iago follows himself and serves neither for love nor duty, he asserts. "Whip me such honest knaves," he says of those who after long and faithful service are cashiered when they are old and useless. He expresses his admiration for the man who appears to perform his duties, but actually attends unflinchingly to his own interests, using his masters only for his own gains. The self-interested man has "soul," Iago declares, and such a man of "soul" is he.

Comment

Iago reveals his true nature to Roderigo, who is incapable of understanding the implications of Iago's self-interested "soul." Logically, Roderigo should conclude that as Iago serves the Moor for his own gains, so must he be serving Roderigo.

The speech shows Iago's contempt for conventional Christian conceptions of the ideal servant. Iago reveals himself as a rebel, an enemy to social order; he has junked the long-standing feudal idea that there is a special beauty and dignity in service to one's master. The idea of service was a Christian principle, devoutly followed throughout the Middle Ages and Renaissance. Based on the biblical paradox of the first being last and the last first, this principle was reflected in one of the papal titles, "the servant of the servant of God." The antithesis of Iago's contemptuous view of service is expressed elsewhere in Shakespeare. Adam, the faithful servant of Oliver in *As You Like It*, reflects "the constant service of the antique world / When service sweat for duty, not for need [reward]."

Roderigo seems inclined to brood over the good fortune of Othello (whom he calls "thick-lips") in winning Desdemona, but Iago calls for action. Rouse Brabantio, Desdemona's father, Iago advises. Let her enraged kinsmen poison Othello's joy and spread plague on his delight. Roderigo agrees.

Immediately, the unseemly pair arrive at Brabantio's house. Iago urges Roderigo to raise a horrible cry as if the whole town were on fire, and he joins him by shouting, "Thieves!" A sleepy and confused Brabantio appears at the window. Roderigo and Iago ask him the condition of his house, knowing that he will be unable to answer their questions. Vulgarly, Iago informs him that his "white ewe" has gone off with a "black ram," meaning, of course, that his daughter has eloped with a dark-skinned Moor or a black man. (Elizabethan made no distinctions between the two.) More respectfully, Roderigo identifies himself, but he is prevented from speaking further by Brabantio's charges of drunkenness and his reminders that Roderigo is unwelcome both to his house and to his daughter.

Patiently, Roderigo attempts to convey his information, but Iago breaks in and, alluding to Othello's race, warns Brabantio that his daughter is being covered by a "Barbary horse" (named from "Barbary" on the coast of North Africa) and that his grandchildren will be "gennets" (black horses).

Comment

Brabantio is a powerful and cultivated citizen, a member of the governing Venetian oligarchy. He has found Roderigo unworthy of his daughter's hand in marriage. Apparently, Roderigo refused to take no for an answer and continued his suit until Brabantio was forced to charge him "not to haunt about my doors." This charge is an appropriate reason for Roderigo's hiring Iago as a go-between.

Shakespeare deliberately contrasts the speech of Roderigo and Iago. Roderigo addresses Brabantio courteously, while Iago uses the bawdy language of the barracks and ale-house.

Brabantio, shocked at this report, asks the "profane" (foul-mouthed) wretch to identify himself. Receiving another virulent report about his daughter and the Moor, Brabantio himself identifies the speaker as a "villain."

Comment

Brabantio's tag for Iago is precisely the one Shakespeare used to describe the character in his "list of actors." The "villain" was a traditional character in native English miracle and morality plays and was frequently called the "Vice" or the "Herod." His function was always to incite mischief or inspire evil, but he was essentially a comic character, for those who rejected the divine goodness inherent in human nature were conventionally regarded as fools. The villain or vice was the greatest fool of all. Those in the old morality plays, like Iago in this scene, used foul language, to the amusement of medieval audiences, and gave the most malicious interpretations possible to the behavior of others.

Iago starts to retaliate the name-calling, but as if out of respect to Brabantio, he cuts himself off and replies, "You are-a senator." Infuriated, Brabantio promises to make Roderigo answer for the insults of the unidentified villain. Still patient and respectful, Roderigo at last gets the opportunity to deliver his message. In a speech ornamented with rhetorical flourishes,

Roderigo informs the senator that his fair daughter has been transported by a common knave, and that, if he knows of this elopement and has consented to it, his informants are guilty of "bold and saucy wrongs." If he does not know of the elopement, then he has wrongly rebuked the informants. With much civility, Roderigo assures Brabantio that he would not trifle over so serious a matter and advises the father to confirm the report of his daughter's revolt.

Addressed in the only language to which he is capable of responding, Brabantio becomes alarmed. He calls for lights, arouses his retainers, and admits that he has had a dream not unlike Roderigo's report. Then he repeats his cry, "Light, I say! light!"

Comment

Brabantio's cry for light is not only a demand for illumination, but part of the texture of light-dark imageries that runs through the first scene. The entire action takes place a night, it should be remembered, but several illuminations occur during the scene. As her father sleeps in darkness and in ignorance, Desdemona, the "white ewe," steals off in the night with Othello, the "black ram." Brabantio soon learns that his "fair" (light) daughter has eloped with the Moor; his call for light appropriately accompanies this enlightenment and the simultaneous illumination or explanation of his dream. Iago too has made substantial revelations on this dark night. He reveals his black hatred for the Moor, his jealousy of Cassio, and his intention to serve his own evil ends.

As Brabantio departs to rouse his household, Iago takes his leave of Roderigo. It is unwholesome, he explains, to be discovered in an action against the Moor, his general. Besides, he tells Roderigo, Brabantio's action against Othello will only "gall him with some check," for Venice needs the Moor to protect its interests in Cyprus. Othello's equal as a military leader cannot be found, Iago maintains, and although he hates the Moor, he must follow and pretend to love him "for necessity of present life." He tells Roderigo to lead Brabantio and his party to the Sagittary (apparently an inn) where Othello can be found.

Comment

Iago says he must follow Othello "for necessity of present life," an ambiguous motive, which may mean "because Othello is needed in the Cyprus wars" or (because Iago has expressed his self-interest so strongly) "because I still need Othello for my own purposes." Either Iago regards Othello as indispensable to the military defense of the Venetian republic, or he wishes Roderigo to think he does. It is not Iago's intention at this time to work the complete destruction of the Moor in order to help Roderigo win Desdemona. He expects only to "gall" (irritate) the Moor, to "poison his delight," or "plague him with flies," and vex his joy.

In his relationship to Roderigo, Iago is like the debtor Shakespeare often describes. When payment is demanded, he satisfies his creditor with a small sum, promising a great deal more than he gives or intends to give. Since Iago cannot turn Desdemona over to Roderigo at the moment, he arranges to "gall" Othello "with some check." Later on, Iago promises, Roderigo may win the lady herself.

As Iago departs, Brabantio returns still wearing his dressing gown; he is attended by servants whose torches light the night. He has checked Desdemona's room, and, indeed, she is gone. Between outbursts of grief for the fate of father, Brabantio questions Roderigo for details. Where did you see her? Was she with the Moor? What did she say? Are they married? When Roderigo expresses the belief that they are married, Brabantio's grief is augmented considerably. How did she get out! he wails. Without waiting for an answer, he accuses his daughter of betraying her blood. Clutching at straws, he seeks an explanation for her betrayal in stories he has read of young girls who have been deceived by charms. Roderigo agrees that he has read stories of such enchantments. Now Brabantio sends for his brother, and in the next breath bemoans the fact that he had refused her to Roderigo.

Comment

Half-mad with grief, Brabantio utters phrases which are difficult to interpret. "Some one way, some another" appears to mean "Some [men are knaves in] one way, some [are knaves in] another." He has saved his daughter from the knave Roderigo only to lose her to a worse husband, Othello. Since the sentence is incomplete, it is possible to fill out the thought in a variety of ways but it is clear that Brabantio's opinion of Roderigo as a son-in-law is only slightly higher than his opinion of the Moor.

At last Brabantio asks where he can find the Moor, and Roderigo agrees to show him the way. Calling for officers and promising to reward Roderigo, Brabantio goes off to find Othello.

SUMMARY

The opening scene establishes the following points:

1. It introduces the main characters of the play, directly through the appearance of Roderigo and Iago,

indirectly through conversation concerning Othello, Desdemona, and Cassio.

2. It establishes the time, place, and action of the play. The first scene takes place in Venice at a time when the Turks were attacking the island of Cyprus, a colony of Venice in 1570; it is suggested that subsequent scenes will take place on Cyprus where Othello must lead his military forces. The action of the play, Iago's plot against Othello, is set in motion by Roderigo's employment of Iago as substitute in his courtship of Desdemona and by Iago's own failure to be appointed as lieutenant.

3. It provides valuable information about Othello before he appears on stage. Othello has eloped with Desdemona, whom Roderigo wants; he is not easily influenced and has appointed Cassio to a post Iago wants; he is the best general available to the Venetian Republic, and he is about to lead an expedition against the Turks.

4. It shows Iago in action as a "self-interested" man, an accomplished instigator, or an "agent provocateur." He has made a gull of Roderigo, bilking him of money without fulfilling the services promised, and he has converted Brabantio into a gad-fly who, serving Iago's purposes as well as his own, will pursue and irritate Othello in his hour of joy.

5. It introduces Brabantio, an influential senator in the Venetian oligarchy and the father of Desdemona, in order to supply background for Desdemona's character. She is a lady of noble lineage, ordinarily

shy and obedient, who, for the sake of the Moor, has abandoned her family and position.

ACT I: SCENE 2

On another street in Venice, Othello, Iago, and several attendants bearing torches appear. Iago is in the middle of a description of his encounter with Brabantio. He tells Othello that Brabantio's remarks so angered him that he felt like killing him but was restrained by the fact that, apart from war, he has never "contriv'd murther," that is, he has never murdered in the heat of passion or for personal reasons. Othello approves of Iago's restraint, but Iago continues to insist on the enormity of the provocation. Brabantio spoke so disparagingly of the Moor's honor that it took all the "godliness" within Iago to **refrain** from harming the man. He warns Othello that Brabantio is extremely powerful in the government of Venice and, like the Duke, has two votes in the senate. (Historically, this would be impossible.) Brabantio will certainly try to divorce the couple and seek every legal means of redress against Othello.

Comment

Having enraged the unwilling father-in law against his daughter's new husband, Iago now attempts to goad Othello into anger against Brabantio. Othello does not take the bait, although Iago persists, stressing Brabantio's vilifications of the Moor, his power in the senate, and his ability to take strong legal action against Othello.

Othello replies that Brabantio may do his worst; he is assured that his military services to the government will outweigh

Brabantio's complaints. Furthermore, Othello asserts, although he does not like boasting, he will make known the fact that he is descended from a royal line. In all due humility, Othello states, his family is equal in honor and rank to the house of Brabantio. He informs Iago that he would not have given up his "unhoused free condition," his bachelor freedom, for anything in the world, except the deepest love.

Comment

Othello's reaction to the potential threat of Brabantio is one of calm and dignity; he has the self-assurance suitable to the commander of men. He has no apologies to make to anyone, and he is not easily angered.

Lights are seen in the darkness as Cassio and several officers with torches arrive. Iago, who is expecting Brabantio, warns Othello to retreat and hide. Othello proudly refuses. Standing his ground, he states confidently, "My parts, my title. and my perfect soul/ Shall manifest me rightly."

Comment

Othello is not only self-assured, but trusts that other men, when presented with the facts, will decide for the truth. Othello's refusal to hide is a mark of his open nature, which will deteriorate later.

Othello now recognizes his lieutenant Cassio and his officers, whom he calls "servants of the Duke" and "friends." Cassio delivers the Duke's summons to Othello. Messengers have been arriving one after the other from the Venetian galleys, and many of the Duke's consuls are already assembled to discuss the emergency. They have sent three times for Othello, who could not be found at his usual lodgings. Othello replies, "'Tis well I am found by you," and promises to join Cassio after he has spent a moment in the house.

Comment

Although he is a fearless man of war, Othello does not like personal conflict. He seems relieved to be found by Cassio rather than Brabantio, for he prefers to be engaged in national rather than domestic strife.

Perplexed at Othellos' delay, Cassio asks Iago what is going on. In a vulgar periphrasis, Iago explains that Othello is married. He is interrupted by Othello's return before he can tell Cassio the name of the bride.

At this point, Brabantio, Roderigo, and armed officers with more torches arrive on the scene. Again, Iago warns Othello of Brabantio's malice. Denouncing Othello as a "thief," Brabantio signals his retainers to draw their swords. An incurable fighter, Iago singles out Roderigo as his special opponent.

Comment

Iago offers to fight Roderigo in order to protect him from harm so that he can continue to make use of his purse, or he wants to kill Roderigo, for whom he has no further use, to avoid paying his debt or fulfilling the promised service. At this point, Iago has not clearly fitted Roderigo into his revenge scheme.

Contemptuously, Othello refuses to respond to Brabantio's violence. "Keep up your bright swords, for the dew will rust them," he advises. Diplomatically, he informs Brabantio, "Good Signior, you shall more command with years / Than with your weapons."

The outraged father loses a stream of invective against Othello. He damns him, calls him an enchanter, insists that the "tender, fair, and happy" Desdemona was so shy of marriage that she shunned the "curled darlings of our nation," that is, the foppish and elegant suitors of the Venetian courts. He insists that Desdemona has been intimidated; why else would he lay her fair head on his "sooty bosom?" The answer must lie in Othello's use of poisonous drugs or black magic, offenses under the law. Brabantio demands Othello's arrest and orders the officers to subdue him if he resists.

Patiently, and with great dignity, Othello assures Brabantio that he has no intention of resisting and agrees to go wherever Brabantio chooses in order to answer his charges. Brabantio chooses prison, where he plans to keep Othello until court convenes to hear the case. Othello then informs Brabantio that he has been summoned by the Duke on business of state and asks how he shall obey both men at the same time. An officer confirms Othello's assertions, and for the first time during this troubled night, Brabantio learns that the Duke is in council. Although he surmises that the state is in danger if the council is assembled at this late hour of the night, Brabantio asserts, "Mine's not an idle cause." He decides to bring his complaint against Othello before the Duke immediately.

Comment

Othello's cool command of the situation in which Iago instigates and Brabantio rages is visible throughout this scene. Notice how tactfully he allows Brabantio to decide that Othello is to be brought to the Duke rather than to prison. The air of self-assurance never leaves Othello during this scene. He is confident that his heroic service, his noble lineage, and his general merits make him deserving of Desdemona and will win him the approval of the senate.

SUMMARY

The scene serves the following purposes:

1. It presents Othello personally for the first time in the play. It helps establish an authentic image of Othello as an alert and poised leader, considerate and diplomatic, but capable of drastic and decisive action. He is a proud man, but not vain-glorious; he knows that boasting is no honor. He is thoroughly convinced of his own integrity ("my perfect soul"), and trusts unquestioningly in the integrity of other men.

2. It shows that the exotic marriage has aroused opposition among conventional but decent people like Brabantio who easily become the tool of malicious men like Iago.

3. It establishes Othello's position as leading military figure in the Venetian state, a position he is careful not to abuse. Unlike Iago, Othello shows his dedication to service and duty.

OTHELLO

. . . .

ACT I: SCENE 3

It is still the same night. The scene now shifts to the Duke's council chamber where the Duke and senators discuss and assess various conflicting reports of the size of the Turkish fleet and its whereabouts. Although they do not fix the enemy's number, the despatches confirm that the enemy fleet is bearing up to Cyprus. The Duke too becomes convinced that Cyprus is in danger, just as a sailor arrives with a message that the Turks are really heading for Rhodes. One senator argues that this is a Turkish trick. Cyprus is more important to the Turks than Rhodes, and it should not be presumed that they would attempt to conquer Rhodes when Cyprus is both easier to win and more profitable to possess. The Duke confirms this belief that Cyprus is the real target. Another messenger arrives hard upon this decision to report that Turkish ships do, indeed, head for Rhodes, but that a second fleet follows behind and steers for Cyprus. The Duke is certain, then, that Cyprus is in danger.

Comment

The council is here discussing various conflicting reports received from the navy, which have already been mentioned by Cassio. Shakespeare frequently relies on the device of the conflicting messages (as in Part 2 *Henry IV*) to establish an atmosphere of danger, uncertainty, and disorder of the sort usually occasioned by war.

At this point, both parties, Othello's and Brabantio's, enter the chamber. Breaking protocol, the Duke first greats Othello with the news that he must be employed at once against the "Ottomans." Then, noticing Brabantio, the Duke apologizes for not seeing him at first. He welcomes Brabantio to court, expressing regret that he had lacked the senator's help this night.

Comment

This small piece of apparently insignificant action, the Duke's welcoming Othello before Brabantio, is laden with meaning. The Duke's breach of protocol (the conventional etiquette of court and state, requiring that the highest ranking man be attended first) reflects the uncertain and disordered atmosphere of the situation; it suggests that social hierarchies and amenities are artificial ones since they are so easily ignored in times of emergency. The Dukes' favoring Othello with the first greeting forecasts his subsequent judgment in favor of Othello and against Brabantio. As Brabantio is not seen first here, so will his cause be "overlooked" later.

Barely returning the Duke's greeting, Brabantio proceeds to outline his daughter has been "abused, stol'n ... and corrupted."

He is so anxious to stress the illegal means by which she was taken, that is, the "spells and medicines" of witchcraft by which she was deceived, that he neglects to name the defendant at first. The Duke promises that Brabantio himself will be allowed to pass judgment on the miscreant, that is, Brabantio will read "the bloody book of law" against his daughter's deceiver "though our proper son / Stood in your action."

Comment

This is neither the first nor last instance in which Shakespeare uses dramatic **irony** and has the character express sentiments which the author knows he will later regret. The Duke's own son does not stand in Brabantio's action, of course, but someone equally important to the Venetian cause, Othello, does.

Much to the regret of the Duke and all the senators, Brabantio points to Othello, the man whom state affairs have brought to court. Although the Duke has believed the charges made by the noble and trusted senator, he now turns to Othello and asks him what he has to say in his own defense. Impatiently, Brabantio insists that Othello has nothing to say but to agree. Nevertheless, Othello speaks. Showing the same tact he had employed with Brabantio before, he does, indeed, begin by agreeing that he has taken Brabantio's daughter. So much is true and no more. Humbly (and eloquently), he asserts his rudeness of speech and his inability to defend himself with the polished smoothness of the civilian. His skill is in "broil and battle," he cleverly reminds the court, and he must rely on the "gracious patience" of the Duke to listen to the "unvarnished tale" of his courtship and by what magic he won Brabantio's daughter.

Comment

Once more Othello's self-possession and directness is explored, this time in his address to the Duke and his court. Despite his claim of "rudeness," he is a most eloquent speaker and is distinctly gifted as a diplomat. He flatters his adversaries, states his own case directly, and does not bother to refute the charges. Rather than deny the crime attributed to him, he wisely stresses his virtues, his skill in combat, which the senators themselves are able to confirm. (An advocate whose plea begins with a truth recognized by all has taken the first step in winning the favor of the jurors.) Paradoxically, Othello offers to explain by what magic he won Desdemona; this is also a diplomatic approach. He chooses not to contradict or deny that he has used "magic," but when the true nature of this "magic" is known, that is, when the paradox is explained, Othello will be vindicated. (Open contradiction is sure to arouse someone's hostility; agreement never fails to win some sympathy.)

Brabantio, however, mistakes Othello's reference to "magic," and passionately interrupts again, repeating the reasoning by which he has concluded that fair, gentle Desdemona must have been drugged. She was a quiet maiden, never bold, and so bashful that she blushed at her own emotions. It is unthinkable that such a timid young lady should oppose her own nature, the modesty befitting her youth, the manners of her country, the honor of her name, and everything else, and fall in love with a man whose very aspect she feared to look at.

Comment

The purpose of the interruption is to describe Desdemona in greater detail just before her appearance. She is, indeed, a maiden of modesty, honor, and all the rest. Yet she has opposed her "nature." Brabantio's reference to nature is a reference to the humanist code of behavior (of the sort drawn up by Baldassare Castiglione in *The Book of the Courtier*), in which persons of a given rank, appearance, education, and sex were expected to conduct themselves with decorum, in accordance with the rules drawn up for that class. Thus, it was "natural" for fair Desdemona, the young daughter of a noble Venetian family, to be shy and retiring, to be obedient to her father, and to marry a man whose race, rank, wealth, and beauty were similar to her own. On the other hand, Castiglione's "perfect lady" always married for love and had the courage to command armies. Desdemona is always the "perfect lady," despite her father's charges.

The Duke responds to Brabantio's outburst by informing him that assertions are not proofs. (He is beginning to suspect that Brabantio's case is unfounded. Notice the parallel situation later when Othello demands proof from Iago of Desdemona's infidelity.) One of the senators asks a direct question. Did he or did he not use drugs? Still, Othello avoids a negative answer and suggests that Desdemona be called to speak before her father. While she is being fetched, Othello offers to recount their courtship.

Comment

When Othello avoids a direct answer to a direct question, he is not being evasive. He seems to feel that the negative answer is the evasive one and prefers to state positive facts, assuming that the listeners will make the right deductions. This is the way he treated the "great ones" of the city who sued for Iago's appointment. Rather than say "no," he advised them that Cassio has been chosen. Here, Othello seems to feel that Brabantio would only be aroused to new violence if Othello denies the charges. Thus, he asks that Desdemona answer her father directly. In this way, Othello hopes to eliminate unnecessary altercation. The matter will be settled finally when Desdemona speaks. In the meantime, he will describe the events which led to their marriage, that is, he will speak truthfully and openly, thereby giving the senators an opportunity to answer their own question. (The audience, moreover, will have the opportunity of learning the events which occurred prior to the opening of the play.)

In a long autobiographical account, Othello then reveals his romantic and adventurous life. He had been a frequent guest in Brabantio's house where he had told his adventures in Desdemona's hearing. For many years, he has been a soldier and has engaged in "battles, sieges, fortunes." He has repeatedly risked his life without question. He had once been captured and made a slave, but had managed to escape. He had been in all sorts of dangerous and mysterious places, vast caves, vacant deserts, high mountains. He has known Cannibals, the "Anthropophagi," and "men whose heads / Do grow beneath their shoulders."

Comment

"Anthropophagi" is another name for cannibals, referring to a particular race of man-eaters. Cannibals are mentioned in Philemon Holland's translation of Pliny's *Natural History* (1601), which may have been Shakespeare's geographical source book. The race of men with misplaced heads is mentioned in Raleigh's Guiana and in other old travelers' books. They are sometimes thought to be Russians who in winter wore huge fur hats which gave travelers the impression that their heads grew in the center of their bodies.

Othello's adventures, the sieges, capture and enslavement, and mysterious travels were of the sort frequently found in the Greek romances, which were in vogue in Shakespeare's time. Because of his strange experiences, Othello is sometimes described as a heroic barbarian who has become civilized, that he is, in fact, a "noble savage." Shakespeare was acquainted with the concept of the "noble savage," which had been described by the French essayist and philosopher, Michel de Montaigne, whom Shakespeare read (and quoted verbatim in The Tempest).

Continuing his narrative, Othello tells how Desdemona was attracted by fragments of his tales, which she had overheard as she came and went about the house. Privately, she requested that he repeat them to her in full. As she listened, she wept over his trials and hardships. Finally, she stated that she would welcome such a man as her suitor. Thus encouraged, Othello proposed marriage. "She loved me for the dangers I had pass'd / And I lov'd her that she did pity them." This was Othello's only witchcraft, he concludes; "Let Desdemona witness it."

Comment

Othello's tale of courtship is not unfamiliar in the history of western literature. Dante's Paolo won Francesca by reading with her the romantic tales of Lancelot and Guinevere. Early puritan tradition, in fact, deplored tales of romance for this very reason, because it was believed that stories of love had the power to subdue and mislead young innocents. There is, indeed, an air of magic and enchantment about the adventures Othello relates, and it is this kind of enchantment, not drugs, that worked the seduction of Desdemona.

Desdemona's pity may be regarded by the modern reader as insufficient reason for falling in love. In medieval and Renaissance tradition, however, the lady's pity was the first requisite for the suitor's cause. It was thought then, and even today, that "pity is akin to love." The traditional lover of romance literature became pale and wan and threatened to die if the lady did not show mercy (pity). Thus, moved to pity, the lady would surrender some token of favor, a kerchief or ring which he would wear on his person. The lover was next ready to deepen her affections by engaging in battle or in tournaments. His success in such ventures would finally win her total esteem and her hand in marriage (or, if she were already married, adultery might follow). After the marriage, the lady became the complete subject of the husband.

Although some steps in the courtship procedure of conventional romances have been eliminated in this play, Desdemona and Othello are lovers in this romantic tradition. Desdemona's courageous and determined manner in the elopement and in the action immediately following, and her subsequent passive submission to Othello's jealousy, are not contradictions of character but are duplication of the dual role (before and after marriage) played by the traditional heroine of romance literature.

At the conclusion of Othello's narrative, Desdemona appears, attended by Iago and several others. The Duke declares that Othello's story would win his daughter too. Before hearing Desdemona's testimony, the Duke asks Brabantio to reconcile himself as best he can to "this mangled matter," to this irregular marriage. Brabantio. however, insists that Desdemona be heard before a decision is made. Gently, he asks his daughter if she knows where her obedience lies. He is clearly unprepared for the answer she gives him. Desdemona replies that her duty is divided. She owes obedience and respect to her father because he gave her life and education, but even for this reason does she now owe obedience to her husband, for her mother had showed her that a woman, once married, must prefer her husband to her father.

Desdemona makes it abundantly clear that she married Othello through her free choice, and, with this declaration, Brabantio's case collapses. Brabantio makes the best of what he considers a bad situation and gives Othello Desdemona apparently with all his heart. But he admits that if Othello did not already possess her, he would do everything in his power to keep her from him.

Comment

Desdemona's first brief statement in the play demonstrates that she is the obedient maiden her father had described. Her brevity speaks for her modesty; at the same time, she demonstrates the independence of mind that characterizes a lady of noble blood with Desdemona's education. She is courageous enough to act on her feelings and has the determination and wit needed to justify her actions.

In a conciliatory speech, the Duke asks Brabantio to smile at his loss, for, in smiling, he prevents the thief from enjoying his discomfort. Wryly, Brabantio suggests that Venice, if it loses Cyprus, may also smile and thus deprive the Turks of their victory. He accepts the Duke's decision reluctantly and finds no ease to his grief in the Duke's words. "I never yet did hear / That the bruised heart was pierced through the ear." Thus, still unreconciled to his daughter's marriage, he asks the Duke to move on the business of the state.

The Duke appoints Othello Commander-in-Chief for the military defense of Cyprus. In no way embarrassed or upset by what has happened, Othello courteously but firmly requests that the state make living arrangements for his wife in accordance with her rank and education. Brabantio refuses to quarter his disobedient daughter, although the Duke has suggested it. Desdemona interposes in her quiet and unaffected way to ask that she may accompany Othello to Cyprus. In doing so, she makes an important declaration about the kind of love she has for this man:

That I did love the Moor to live with him, My downright violence and storm of fortunes, May trumpet to the world. My heart's subdu'd Even to the very quality of my lord. I saw Othello's visage in his mind, And to his honors and his valiant parts Did I my soul and fortunes consecrate. So that, dear lords, if I be left behind, A moth of peace, and he go to the war, The rights for which I love him are bereft me, And I a heavy interim shall support By his dear absence. Let me go with him.

Othello adds his own request to Desdemona's. He does not ask that Desdemona be with him simply to satisfy his rights as a husband, "but to be free and bounteous to her mind." Love will not interfere with Othello's responsibilities for the conduct of the war.

Comment

Othello's request that Desdemona accompany him for her sake rather than his own has been interpreted to mean that Othello is sexually impotent. Othello speaks of "the young affects / In me defunct" in regard to "heat" or sexual desire. Later in the play (II. iii. 354), Iago refers to Othello's "weak function" with which Desdemona "may play the god." One critic, horrified by miscegenation, insists that the marriage must be platonic. The common sense position is that this is a real marriage, that Desdemona, in referring to "the rites for which I love him," frankly speaks of the marriage rites, the consummation of the marriage. Othello is not a young man by Elizabethan standards, where the average age of death was forty-five. His sexual drive has been modified by his advanced years but not curtailed. Shakespeare stresses in Desdemona's and Othello's speeches both the spiritual affinity which exists between the lovers and the physical attachment they have made to one another. Desdemona "did love the Moor to live [physically] with him," but her heart was completely vanquished "even to the very [spiritual] quality of my lord." Othello, of course, wishes to assure the senate that he will not stint in his military efforts merely because his wife is with him.

The request of the newly wedded couple is granted by the Venetian senate, and the Duke affirms to Brabantio that "Your son-in-law is far more fair than black."

As the senate adjourns, Othello is given meaningful advice by the first senator and by Brabantio. The senator urges Othello to use Desdemona well, while Brabantio warns: "She has deceived her father, and may thee." Othello answers, "My life upon her faith!"

Comment

Each of these remarks is an example of Shakespeare's "**foreshadowing**" technique. Othello will not use Desdemona well, we will learn shortly. Brabantio's warning, which Othello belies at this point, will be remembered and believed later, and

Othello will give up his life as a result of Desdemona's fidelity. It is the discovery of her loyalty which makes Othello kill himself.

When the Duke and senators leave, Othello entrusts Iago with Desdemona's safe voyage and asks him to have Emilia, his wife, wait on her. Then, with only an hour left to attend to love and business, Othello departs with his bride.

Comment

Desdemona, whom we have met for the first time in this scene, reveals herself as an aristocratic girl, who observes all the **conventions** but who, at the same time, has a determined mind of her own. She had handled Brabantio with tact and firmness. She is a little shy in making her request to go to Cyprus with Othello ("let me find a charter in your voice / T'assist my simpleness"), but she makes it gracefully and forcibly. Her subsequent passivity in regard to Othello is explained by the traditional submissiveness of wives to their husbands which Desdemona has learned from her mother. It may be that her heart was "subdued" too completely, that she lacked a certain needed **realism** in order to cope with his suspicions. One of the most potent effects of this tragedy is Desdemona's suffering under Othello's later tyranny. At this point in the play, however, he gives her freedom; he is "free and bounteous to her mind."

Roderigo has witnessed the entire action and when the council chamber is cleared, he turns to Iago and announces that he is going to drown himself. To live without Desdemona would be torment, and although he is ashamed of his foolishness, he admits that he has not the "virtue" (an inherent power of character) to amend the foolishness.

Anxious to save his dupe, Iago responds heatedly. In all twenty-eight years, he has never met a man who knew how to love himself. Personally, Iago argues, he would rather be an ape (a creature without reason) than kill himself for a woman. As for "virtue" (the naturally endowed powers Roderigo says he lacks), we are what we will ourselves to be, Iago asserts. If we had not this will, we'd be nothing more than beasts, subject to "carnal stings" and "unbitted lusts." Fortunately however, man has reason to cool his lusts. Love is only a form of lust, Iago tells the incredulous Roderigo; it is a condition that exists only with the permission of the will.

Comment

In a curious perversion of puritan logic, Iago reveals that he is a man of will (mind rather than feeling). Unfortunately, he confuses love with lust and negates both forces. Lust is to be overcome in order to achieve noble deeds (as Othello does), but love is universal and absolute. The love of woman is the bottom of the ladder to heaven, for only through human love experienced in youth can man learn to know the divine love of God; so thought some of the humanists of the high Renaissance.

Iago is a self-interested man who loves himself rather than woman. (He will never get to heaven.) We learn, in addition, that he is twenty-eight, that he has found all men to be fools, that he believes in the essential corruption of human nature and in the supremacy of will. Iago is not subject to the demands of the flesh, and he does not believe in the absolute existence of love.

Iago's cold philosophy makes little impression on Roderigo, but when Iago tells the foolish lover again and again to put money in his purse to follow the wars, and to wait for Desdemona to tire of the Moor, Roderigo's hopes begin to rise. Iago assures him that love which begins violently ends in the same way, and that Desdemona, finished with the old Moor, will begin to look for a young lover. He promises that Roderigo will enjoy Desdemona yet, if Iago's wits and "all the tribe of hell" (which apparently serves as inspiration to his wit) are any match for the barbarous Moor and the "supersubtle" (sophisticated) Venetian, Desdemona. Once more resolved to live, Roderigo agrees to follow Iago's advice and sets off at once to sell his land.

Comment

Iago associates himself with the traditional Vice of morality literature in at least two ways. First, he asserts that he does not believe in love; he sees it only as the permission of the will to the lusts of the body. This is truly a satanic notion, for love between man and woman was regarded by Christians of Shakespeare's world as the human version and manifestation of divine love, a love which had absolute existence and could not be "willed" by man. Secondly, Iago suggests that "all the tribe of hell" may assist his wit (intellect), implying thereby that he himself is an instrument of hell.

Left alone, Iago utters the first soliloquy of the play. He states that he has only saved Roderigo for the sake of his purse and for the fun that the foolish man gives him. Otherwise, he would not waste his time expending his hard-earned knowledge of human nature on such a "snipe" as Roderigo. Reaffirming his hatred for Othello, Iago then says rather strangely that he suspects the Moor of having relations with his own wife (Emilia), yet he doesn't know or seem to care whether or not his suspicion has any foundation.

Comment

A soliloquy is a **convention** of the Shakespearean theater in which the character speaks his thoughts aloud. Since there is no dramatic interaction taking place during a soliloquy, it is generally presumed that the character is speaking the truth. The soliloquy tends to explain the paradoxical behavior of a character. Thus, Iago, who does not mean what he says, whose feelings are often contrary to his actions in the play, is given the largest number of soliloquies in the play; while open-natured Othello, who means what he says, for the most part, does not have to explain himself in the soliloquy convention.

Regarding Emilia and Othello's adultery, Shakespeare seems to be suggesting that malice precedes cause in a character like Iago and that his malice can feed on false as well as true reports. We learn later that suspicion is begotten and feeds upon itself. This seems to be precisely what Iago is demonstrating here.

Next, Iago works out a plot against Othello, which he formulates as he speaks. Since the Moor has faith in his ancient (Iago), he will be inclined to believe Iago when he suggests that Cassio is too familiar with Desdemona. According to Iago, Othello is an "ass" because he has a "free and open nature." Othello thinks others are as honest as he "that but seem to be so." Delighted by the plan he has just devised, Iago exclaims, "Hell and night / Must bring this monstrous birth to the world's light."

Comment

Iago's malicious plot is purposefully associated with hell and with unnatural "monstrous" deeds engendered there, which are too heinous for the light of day and may be enacted only in the dark of night. Iago's final lines produce the most horrific of the dark images that blight the first act and forecast doom to the heroic, idealistic lovers, Othello and Desdemona.

SUMMARY

In this scene we have passed beyond ordinary dramatic exposition to what is technically called "the growth of the action." Conflict has been foreshadowed in relation to the marriage by the arguments of Brabantio, who has left us with an ominous portent: "Look to her, Moor, if thou hast eyes to see. / She has deceiv'd her father, and may thee." (Iago is to repeat this idea in a later context: "She did deceive her father, marrying you," in III, iii, 207.) Dramatically, the scene establishes the following points:

1. It makes clear the stature of Othello as a leader, a man of dignity and widespread respect.

2. It explains Othello's romantic and adventurous background and how very plausible was the love that developed between Othello and Desdemona.

3. It shows us the beauty and charm of Desdemona, and her capacity for independent action.

4. It stresses the marriage as basically one of intellectual and spiritual compatibility.

5. It brings into sharp contrasting focus the idealistic and inspiring qualities of the wedded couple with the malice and cynicism of Iago.

6. It shows the "monstrous birth" of Iago's plot to destroy the unsuspecting couple.

OTHELLO

....

ACT II: SCENE 1

Some weeks have passed. The action moves on to Cyprus. Montano, a leading citizen of Cyprus, discusses the war with two gentlemen. Montano is satisfied that the Turkish fleet has either sought refuge somewhere or has been destroyed in the course of a terrific storm that has been raging. A third gentleman brings news that the Turkish fleet has, indeed, suffered serious losses and that Cassio has arrived in Cyprus. Othello, who has been given the full powers of governor of the island, is still at sea. The gentleman reports that Cassio is worried about Othello's safety. Montano expresses his hope for Othello's safe return, for he once served under the Moor and found him to be a perfect commander.

Cassio now joins the group. Having heard Montano speak of Othello, he thanks him for his praise. He assures Montano that Othello's ships is a strong one and his pilot well-skilled; he has good hopes for the governor's safety. A second ship is sighted, and, as Montano and Cassio await a report on its passengers, Cassio tells his companion that the Moor is married to "a maid / That paragons description and wild fame; / One that excels the quirks of blazoning pens."

Comment

Cassio has already been described as "bookish" by his rival, Iago. Now he demonstrates this bookishness in elaborate praise of Desdemona. His **diction** is elegant and his manner courtly; neither Iago nor Othello, both practical men of war, will appreciate or understand his courtly ways with Desdemona.

Desdemona's ship has arrived. She is accompanied by Iago, Roderigo, and Emilia. Desdemona thanks Cassio for his effusive welcome and expresses her fear over Othello's delayed arrival. A bantering conversation ensues when Cassio kisses Emilia's hand in greeting and renders her speechless. But she finds her tongue when Iago describes her as a chiding wife and she warrants that he shall never write her praise. Iago goes on to defame the female sex in general. Encouraged by the company, he recites several proverbial jests about the frailty of women. Everyone takes them in good humor, including Desdemona, who calls Iago a "profane and liberal counsellor." Cassio is forced to admit that Iago speaks truthfully and to the point, and suggests that Desdemona will find greater merit in Iago as a soldier than as a scholar. Cassio next extends the courtesy of aristocratic hand-kissing to Desdemona, as Iago looks on. In an "aside" (a stage whisper, another **convention** of the Elizabethan theater, in which the speech is intended only for the audience's hearing), Iago comments: "He takes her by the palm. Ay, well said, whisper! With as little a web as this will I ensnare as great a fly as Cassio."

Comment

As a polished Florentine gentleman following the new fashion of Renaissance courtesy, Cassio kisses hands. Iago's "limericks" or anti-female verses express his true view of women but Cassio and Desdemona interpret his behavior as that of a typical rough-hewn soldier, somewhat extrovert and vulgar, but with a heart of gold. Iago's stage whisper indicates his truly sinister (and quasi puritanical) nature; he is never at rest, never relaxed. Even during this exchange of social pleasantries, he is planning to make an evil situation out of a gentle courtesy.

At last Othello arrives. He embraces Desdemona and expresses his supreme happiness at this moment of reunion. She is his "soul's joy." "If after every tempest come such calms / May the winds blow till they have waken'd death!" Othello then expresses the fear that such great contentment as he feels just now cannot come twice in a single lifetime.

Comment

Othello's expression of fear is an example of "tragic foreshadowing," a technique used sparingly but effectively by Shakespeare. We have had a previous example when Brabantio has warned about the possibility of Desdemona deceiving Othello (I.iii.294). Critics often speak of such statements as "ironic." The **irony** here lies in the fact that Othello has spoken much more prophetically than he had any reason to suspect in fearing that such contentment will not come again.

Desdemona replies with a hopeful picture of a future full of tenderness and love. Othello responds by putting his hand upon his heart which has almost stopped beating through the weight of emotion. Kissing her, he says that kisses ought to be the greatest "discords" they may ever be forced to experience. Iago, looking on, reveals his satanic thoughts in another "aside." Grimly jesting on his undeserved sobriquet, "honest Iago," he picks up Othello's musical **metaphor**: "O, you are well tun'd now! / But I'll set down the pegs that make this music / As honest as I am." Prattling happily about the victory, the good people of Cyprus, and his joyous reunion with his bride, Othello leads Desdemona off to his castle.

We now have a long chorus-like dialogue between Iago and Roderigo, in which Iago assures his dupe that Desdemona loves Cassio. Iago pours out his envy, spleen, and disdain for the marriage of Othello and Desdemona. He again reveals his contempt for sex, and he reduces all human relationships to the lowest common denominator. Iago pictures Desdemona as an animal of aggressive sexuality. Dulled by the "act of sport," and obviously promiscuous as all women are, she will seek a handsome man to renew her interest in love. Othello, according to Iago, is not physically attractive, and Desdemona, who already showed her imbecility in choosing such a braggart, will soon be bored with him. Here is where Cassio will come in, for he has what women of "folly and green minds look after." In fact, Iago declares, "the woman hath found him already." Roderigo objects; he cannot believe any such thing; Desdemona is "full of most blessed condition." "Blessed fig's end!" Iago shouts; "the wine she drinks is made of grapes." (She is only human.) Besides, she indulges in courtesies, which are prologue to lust.

Comment

Shakespeare has here made an important contribution to the characterization of villainy, of the evil man. The villain here is not a man of vicious habits. Neither a drunkard nor a philanderer, but a man of iron self-control, with a very low emotional temperature. As long as they have warm hearts, Shakespeare sympathizes with sinful individuals who succumb to the vices of the flesh (e.g. Falstaff). But Shakespeare's evil man is totally unsympathetic. Iago is egocentric and without fellow-feeling; he is cool and self-disciplined; he has no use for women.

Next, Iago broaches his plan to get Cassio out of the way by having Roderigo provoke an incident which will put Cassio in a bad light as an undisciplined officer. With Cassio ruined, Roderigo will be better able to effect his purposes (Iago's actually).

When Roderigo departs, Iago, in a second soliloquy, reviews his accomplishments of the day and his plans for the future. He reveals his belief that Cassio actually loves Desdemona. He decides that her love for Cassio will make a likely and credible story (but it will only be a story). Whatever else Iago feels about the Moor, he does admit that Othello will make a good husband, for he "is of a constant, loving, noble nature." Iago then restates his self-induced idea that Othello may have committed adultery with Emilia and decides to seduce Desdemona himself in order to be "even'd with him, wife for wife." Considering the possible failure of his plan to seduce Desdemona, Iago devises an alternate plan. If the seduction fails, he will make Othello incurably jealous of Cassio. Of course, the fool Roderigo must play his part properly if Cassio is to fall into Iago's power, an idea which appeals to Iago. Next Iago expresses his belief that Cassio (if he tried) could seduce Emilia. Finally, Iago gloats over the thanks he will receive from Othello "for making him egregiously an ass," that is, he envisions how Othello will thank him for falsely informing on Desdemona and Cassio.

These are the evil conceptions formulating in Iago's mind. Iago realizes that his plan for revenge is only roughly outlined, but he states his intention of working out the details as the events occur: "'Tis here [in his head], but yet confus'd." Knavery is unpredictable, Iago says; its course becomes clearer only after it is put into effect.

Comment

Although this second soliloquy has caused critics to charge Shakespeare with inconsistency in the characterization of Iago, it is possible to reach a satisfactory explanation of Iago's remarks. In this soliloquy, Iago is engaged in the act of thinking; he is making tentative and alternative plans; he is testing and checking his ideas for their probability and workability. His thoughts are still unorganized, and they are presented in the manner in which they occur to him, a manner resembling the "internal monologue" technique used by modern novelists. If we place these thoughts into logical order and fill in some ideas which are understood but not spoken, we get the following results: Iago begins with a single overall aim, to revenge himself against Othello. Next, he examines certain given factors. These are his real beliefs: that Cassio loves Desdemona, that all women are fickle and adulterous, that Desdemona, being a woman, is potentially adulterous, that Othello will be a satisfactory husband (consequently, Desdemona may not become adulterous), and that Roderigo is a willing but not necessarily an able accomplice. Now the question for Iago is how to work his revenge within this given framework. The soliloquy explores possible answers to this question. Not all the statements in it are statements of fact.

Some are possibilities, such as "For I fear Cassio with my nightcap too." This means that Cassio is so young, attractive, well-educated ("bookish"), eloquent, and courteous, that Iago himself, recalling no doubt that Emilia was speechless when Cassio kissed her hand only moments ago, fears his potential powers over Emilia. The Moor, therefore, may very well believe Iago's trumped-up charges against Cassio and Desdemona.

SUMMARY

This scene has succeeded in showing the following developments as part of the "growth of action":

1. A transition is effected between Acts I and II, moving the scene of action from Venice to Cyprus and bridging several weeks of time from the eve of the Turkish war to the day of victory.

2. Emilia and several minor characters are introduced in this scene. Emilia, a sharp-tongued wife according to Iago's report, is a spirited wench. Cassio, who made a brief appearance prior to this scene, is developed here as a courteous and eloquent gentleman whose manners suggest his own downfall to Iago.

3. Othello and Desdemona, reunited on Cyprus, have every reason to look forward to a fruitful and happy future. Their reunion is a moment of sheer and complete happiness. Whatever may happen in the future, they have at least known this.

4. With poisonous compulsiveness shown in his cynical contempt for mankind, Iago is seen formulating his plans for revenge, using Roderigo as a tool in his device.

ACT II: SCENE 2

This is scarcely a scene at all. On a street in Cyprus, an official messenger or "herald" reads a proclamation that there is to be a public festival, with free food and drink for all, to celebrate the utter destruction of the Turkish fleet. Moreover, Othello's marriage is to be honored with dancing, bonfires, and other sport.

Comment

Such celebrations were customarily held after victories. Dramatically, this scene of less than fifteen lines prepares us for festivities (most of which will not be shown) during which military discipline will be relaxed. Obviously, there will be drinking and disorder in the camp on this night, making it possible for Iago to work his plot against Cassio more effectively.

The call for bonfires and revels between five and eleven at night reminds us of Iago's first soliloquy when his plot was first "engendered" and Iago proclaimed, "Hell and night / Must bring this monstrous birth to the world's light." We may easily imagine the ensuing festival as a kind of Walpurgisnacht (a drinking feast held on the eve of May 1 in honor of St. Walpurgis, during which, it was believed, witches rode the night to some appointed evil rendezvous.) The proclamation of the feast serves as an omen of an contrast to the stark tragedy which follows it.

ACT II: SCENE 3

Othello, Desdemona, Cassio, and attendants are present as the scene opens in a hall of Othello's castle. Othello admonishes Cassio in "honorable step" (moderation). The festival should not outrun discretion, Othello cautions, and guard duty is to be observed as usual. Cassio promises to instruct Iago accordingly and to supervise the frolics personally. Othello concludes the interview, observing that "Iago is most honest," a good man for the job.

Comment

Despite his brief appearance at this point, Othello exhibits his special wisdom as commander of the army. He himself does not partake of the more riotous aspects of the festivities; he has his charge as governor constantly in mind, believes in moderation and in caution, and in delegating authority to men he trusts.

Unfortunately, it is this trusting nature which brings about the misfortunes of the night. Othello's words and Cassio's answers are laden with tragic **irony**. At Iago's instigation, Cassio will forget moderation and discretion, and will imbibe too much. His personal supervision of the watch will be the most undesirable thing this night, and Iago, of course, is not honest at all.

Iago reports to Cassio just after Othello leaves with his wife and attendants. At Cassio's suggestion that they begin their watch, Iago protests it is too early to renew their duties; it is only ten o'clock. Othello's departure should not be a sign that the feast is over, Iago states; the general has left early because he is anxious to enjoy his wife. "He hath not yet made wanton the night with her," Iago explains, "and she is sport for Jove."

Comment

Iago's explanation for Othello's early retirement on the night of the feast is an ambiguous one. It has been interpreted to mean that Othello has not yet consummated his marriage to Desdemona because of his hasty embarkation from Venice on the eve of the Turkish attack. It may also mean that Othello has not yet enjoyed his wife since his arrival on Cyprus earlier that day. In either case, Iago is alluding to the connubial rites, which he feels Othello is anxious to perform.

Cassio responds to Iago's vulgar description of Desdemona with several courtly phrases of his own. She is "exquisite"; she is "a most fresh and delicate creature"; she is "perfection." Iago, on the other hand, finds her "full of game," "a parley to provocation," "an alarum to love."

Comment

The blunt military language of Iago serves as a contrast to the polite speech of the educated Florentine, Cassio. Cassio seems to disapprove of Iago's metaphors, but he sees them as characteristic expressions of the practical soldier and does not take them as insults to Desdemona. Iago may be trying, without much success, to suggest her availability to Cassio, who Iago believes is in love with her.

Pleading with Cassio not to hurry to the military watch, Iago invites him to a "stope of wine" with "a brace of Cyprus gallants." Cassio declines, saying he has already had one watered glass of wine tonight and that it has not agreed with him. Iago insists; it is a "night of revels," and besides, the gallants are waiting outside for his company. With characteristic politesse, Cassio goes at once to greet the gallants, leaving Iago alone momentarily.

In a brief soliloquy, Iago expresses his belief that if he can succeed in getting Cassio to take one more drink, the lieutenant will become as quarrelsome as a young lady's dog. Now Roderigo (who cannot always be counted on to play his part properly) is already drunk (and thus, oddly enough more reliable) and has been appointed to guard duty that night. In addition, Iago has plied with wine three Cypriots, mettlesome young men, sensitive to "honor," who are also to keep watch. Amid this "flock of drunkards," it would seem easy to provoke Cassio to some offensive action, which would arouse all of Cyprus against him (and make his dismissal mandatory). As Cassio returns with Montano, several gentlemen, and a servant with wine, Iago's reflections break off with the lines:

If consequence do but approve my dream, My boat sails freely, both with wind and stream

Comment

In addition to Cassio's inability to drink and Roderigo's unreliability unless he is drunk, the touchy relationship between the proud Cypriots and their Venetian governors is another factor in Iago's plot. Iago has an uncanny skill for detecting everyone's foibles and for incorporating them into his malicious designs.

It should be noted that Iago calls his thoughts "my dream" and that he is not certain that his "dream" or plot will work as he hopes. The statements in Iago's soliloquies, therefore, are not statements of "fact" but of hope and of probability. When some of Iago's ideas are not subsequently enacted in the play, this should be taken to mean that Iago's revenge plot is working out according to one set of plans and that alternate schemes have not been necessary. So, for example, although Iago says he will try to seduce Desdemona, he never actually makes such an attempt because it would not suit the particular "knavery" that is set in motion during the feast night.

Montano now insists that Cassio should have a drink, and Cassio, caught up by the spirit of the feast, accepts. Iago swings into action, singing two boisterous songs, which he has learned in England, a country of expert drinkers. Iago has skillfully turned the social occasion into a drinking party.

Comment

The drinking party, Iago's ditties, and his jokes about England operate as a comic interlude between the more serious scenes of the play. The Elizabethan audience was a heterogeneous one, and Shakespeare devised his plays to suit the tastes of all. Thus, many of his plays have comic sub-plots underscoring the serious events of the main plot. Perhaps, in no other play was Shakespeare more successful in uniting comedy with tragedy as in Othello. Here there is no sub-plot to interrupt the progress of the main events (unless Roderigo's suit may regarded as one); instead, there are relevant interludes which have direct bearing on the main section. Iago's anti-female verses, recited during the first interview between Cassio and Desdemona, have a similar function in the play. They provide comic entertainment in themselves and, at the same time, work as ironic commentaries on the plot. The hackneyed (and Iago's personal) belief that all women are fickle and adulterous is the basis of Iago's revenge scheme; the drinking party with Cassio is the first stage of the scheme.

Cassio begins to show the effects of wine and is very self-conscious about it. He begins to talk about religious salvation. Inadvertently, he throws a barb at Iago (who has suffered by

Cassio's promotion) when he says "the lieutenant is to be saved before the ancient." (This is, ironically, also true.) "Do not think, gentlemen, I am drunk. This is my ancient; this is my right hand, and this is my left," Cassio raves, as he staggers away from the party.

Montano (who holds his liquor well) suggests that the party return to duty and mount the watch. Assuming a pitying air, Iago tells Montano that Cassio, "this fellow that is gone before," is really a fine military man. Unfortunately, his drinking vice is as great as his virtue as a soldier. Othello puts too much trust in him, Iago fears. Someday, Cassio's drunkenness will cause the whole isle of Cyprus to shake.

Alarmed over the safety of his island, the Cypriot gentleman Montano asks, "But is he often thus?" With mock reluctance, Iago replies that Cassio frequently drinks himself to sleep, for if he is sober, he will stay awake all day and night. Montano, now more concerned, suggests that Othello be informed of Cassio's habits; perhaps the general takes his lieutenant too much on appearances and does not penetrate his real deficiency.

Comment

Montano makes another ironic pronouncement. Othello does, indeed, believe the appearance or outward behavior of men, but it is Iago who should be mistrusted, of course, not Cassio.

Roderigo appears briefly, and Iago secretly orders him to follow Cassio. He departs at once. Meanwhile, Montano continues his ironic commentary on the Moor's favored officer. It is dangerous for Cassio to be in command; the Moor ought to be informed, Montano decides. With his usual duplicity, Iago asserts that he loves Cassio and would not inform on him for all "this fair island."

Comment

Cleverly, Iago shifts the burden of playing informer to Montano, who for the sake of Cyprus, "this fair island," presumably could do what Iago, a Venetian, would not. Iago pretends to value the interests of his friend Cassio above the interests of Cyprus. It will not be necessary for Montano to speak to Othello, however, for in a moment Cassio will seal his own doom.

It is sometimes supposed that Iago, acting as a kind of chorus or commentator on the events in the play, knows of Cassio's imminent disgrace and dismissal and is preparing Montano (for the sake of Cyprus) to protest his reappointment, should Othello decide to reinstate the dishonored lieutenant. But if Iago is a prophetic chorus, he should know that the reappointment will never take place, just as he knows about the forthcoming disgrace. It is more reasonable to suppose that Iago is merely assuring himself of a new dupe should Roderigo fail to incite Cassio to work his own disgrace. In addition, his suggestion of the danger to Cyprus from Cassio's drunkenness serves as dramatic **foreshadowing**. The author knows what is coming next, but Iago does not.

Noise suddenly erupts from "within" (offstage), and Cassio appears, driving Roderigo before him. Angrily, Cassio tells Montano that this rogue, this rascal (Roderigo), has tried to teach him his duty. Roderigo and Cassio come to blows. Montano intervenes and Cassio threatens him roughly. As Montano and Cassio tussle, Iago slyly directs Roderigo to run off and rouse the town. Iago next turns to the combatants and makes a feeble effort to break up the fight. Hearing bells in the distance, Iago pretends to wonder who rang them. Belatedly, Iago warns Cassio to desist or he will awaken the town and be disgraced forever.

Having heard the bells, Othello arrives at once. Montano exclaims that he has been wounded. (Some editions of the play indicate that Montano faints at this point, but in view of Othello's subsequent line, "Hold for your lives," it is apparent that Montano, although wounded, is still on his feet and doing battle. "Faint" may be a misreading for "feint" - (a movement with a sword.)

His sense of military propriety shocked, Othello cries, "Hold"; Iago echoes his command. Are we like the Turks, to kill ourselves when heaven has prevented our enemies from killing us? Othello demands. He reminds the combatants that they are Christians, not barbarians, and warns, "He that stirs next . . . / . . . dies upon his motion." Acting swiftly and decisively, Othello orders that the bells be silenced, for it will frighten the inhabitants of Cyprus out of their senses. Next, he turns to "honest Iago," whose face he finds "dead with grieving." He charges Iago "on his love" for his general to identify the trouble-maker.

Comment

Although attention has been focused on Othello since his arrival on the scene, Iago's presence should not be overlooked for a moment. He parrots Othello's command that the fighters hold, even though they are likely to obey the general's first word. During Othello's speech, Iago has apparently donned an expression of grief, parodying the general's reproach with appropriate grimaces. In short, he has behaved like a comic "yes-man."

Iago replies that he cannot identify the miscreant. Only moments ago, he reports, Montano, Cassio, and all were as friendly as bride and groom undressing for bed. (Iago slyly alludes to what he supposes Othello and Desdemona were doing before the bells sounded, hoping to infuriate the Moor all the more because he has been disturbed at such a moment.)

With feigned innocence, Iago disclaims any knowledge of the cause of this "opposition bloody." Turning to the others, Othello pursues his inquiry. Cassio asks pardon; he cannot speak. Next, Othello asks Montano, reputed in his youth for his serious and peaceful nature, why he has suddenly turned "night-brawler." But Montano, who has been seriously wounded in the fight, finds it difficult to speak. He refers Othello to Iago for the explanation and intimates that he has fought only in self-defense.

Othello is annoyed with everyone's reticence and warns them not to anger him further. Echoing the Duke's promise to Brabantio to punish his own son if it is required by justice, Othello promises to punish the offender though he turned out to be his own twin brother. The crime of disturbing the peace is a serious one, for Cyprus is still a "town of war," and its people are still anxious and fearful over the dangers they have just escaped. To hold a private quarrel "in night, and on the court and guard of safety? 'Tis monstrous," Othello declares. "Iago, who began 't?" the Moor demands.

Comment

Othello uses the same words to describe the nocturnal disturbances raised in the "town of war" as Iago had used to describe the revenge plot he had devised at the end of the first act. Both are monstrous acts that take place in the night.

BRIGHT NOTES STUDY GUIDE

Thus, the "private quarrel" and Iago's revenge-plot are linked metaphorically, emphasizing the fact that they are literally one and the same thing. When Othello turns to Iago to repeat his questions about who began the fight, an ironic touch is added to the scene, for clearly the answer is Iago himself.

Montano, too, urges that Iago tell the truth, reminding him that if he shows partiality to Cassio because of personal friendship or official ties, he is no soldier. Iago admits that Montano has hit home. He would rather lose his tongue than use it against Cassio. However, he is convinced that speaking truth could not injure the lieutenant. He describes how he and Montano were engaged in conversation when Cassio came running in with sword drawn, pursuing some fellow (Roderigo, whom Iago pretends he does not know). Montano interposed, attempting to restrain Cassio, while Iago pursued the other fellow to prevent his cries from terrifying the town. The fellow eluded him, but hearing sword-play and Cassio's swearing (as he had never heard him do before), Iago returned to find Montano and Cassio at blows. This is all he knows, Iago states. Damning Cassio finally in a pretended defense, Iago suggests that surely Cassio must have endured from his victim some "strange indignity, / Which patience could not pass." Othello acknowledges Iago's desire to ameliorate Cassio's guilt. Turning to Cassio, Othello informs him that though he loves him, he relives him of his duties as an officer forever.

Desdemona (who has heard the disturbance) arrives to inquire about the matter, but Othello puts her off and sends her back to her room. Advising Montano that he personally will attend to his wounds, he has him taken away. Next he orders Iago to placate any Cypriots who have been disturbed by the commotion. Such is the soldier's life, he tells Desdemona.

Othello is especially concerned about restoring and maintaining order in Cyprus now that the war with the Turks is over. He shows the same concern any general would have with the discipline of his men and with the opinion of the inhabitants of occupied territory. Iago is aware of Othello's responsibilities and interpolates his own concern for the town during his testimony, thereby confirming Othello's faith in him. Since the hearing is held in a public place, in a town under martial law, Othello has no other choice than to dismiss Cassio even though he loves him.

Iago and Cassio are now left alone. Apparently Cassio has begun to groan, for Iago now asks him if he is hurt. Cassio replies that he is hurt past all surgery and begins to confide in him at once. Cassio is distraught by the public loss of his reputation. What's reputation, asks Iago, but nothing at all? (He is going to tell Othello in a later scene that reputation is practically everything.) Cassio is being punished as a matter of military policy; there is no hard feeling behind it. To his satisfaction, Iago learns that Cassio cannot identify Roderigo. The drinking had blurred his mind, and he can remember the events of the night only as "a mass of things." Iago tells Cassio to stop worrying about his drunkenness: "You or any man living may be drunk at a time." He advises him to try to get his post back through Desdemona's influence, "for she holds it a vice in her goodness not to do more than is requested." Cassio is very grateful to "honest" Iago for his constructive advice and leaves Iago, who must attend to his guard duty.

Once alone, Iago expresses his thought in another soliloquy. Alluding to his conversation with Cassio, he gloats, "And what's he then that says I play the villain?" Doesn't he give Cassio the most probable advice, freely and honestly showing him the way to win Othello's approval again? Desdemona can easily be made to support a cause, for she is as bounteous as the four elements (fire, air, earth, and water), which are free to all. In turn, Desdemona can win over Othello, for his "soul is so enfetter'd to her love," that he will grant her every wish. "How am I then a villain?" Iago asks again with melodramatic heaviness and malicious delight. He addresses himself to the "Divinity of hell" and compares his methods to those of devils, who, when they wish to entice a soul to "blackest sins," first put on "heavenly shows" of virtue.

Planning his next move, Iago decides that, while Desdemona appeals to Othello to recall Cassio to his post, Iago will pour the libel into Othello's ear that she is motivated to aid Cassio by adulterous lust. Iago's eventual triumph will be the destruction of all his enemies through Desdemona's virtue: "And out of her own goodness make the net / That shall enmesh them all."

Comment

No one has called Iago villain, but the Elizabethan audience most assuredly thought it. In fact, the audience may have very well hissed and shouted names at Iago's more reprehensible deeds. Traditionally, the villain was regarded as a comic figure, and Iago is an especially good comedian. In addition to his bawdy, antifemale jests, his robust drinking songs, his mockeries and grimaces, Iago expresses the habitual astonishment of deadpan innocence that must have been very funny to Shakespeare's audience. For example, when Cassio says he doesn't remember what happened when he was drunk, Iago exclaims, "Isn't possible?" (III.iii.286.) Later, when Othello says farewell to tranquility and war, Iago responds with the same feigned innocence, "Isn't possible, my lord?" (III.iii.358). This sardonic humor in the face of others' sufferings underscores Iago's demonic cruelty, while at the same time his humor relieves momentarily the ugliness of the cruelty.

Once more Iago displays his ability to identify the weaknesses of others: Othello's compliance to Desdemona's wishes is his "weak function." Iago is equally good at identifying virtue (which he regards as another form of weakness). Desdemona's bounteous nature is the goodness, which will make the net to ensnare Iago's enemies.

The prospect of destroying goodness through goodness affords Iago particular satanic satisfaction. His invocation to the "Divinity of Hell," his diabolically perverse logic, and his equation of his own methods with those of the devils, serve as additional reminders that Iago friend-like himself.

Roderigo enters, interrupting Iago's reflections, and declares his impatience to win Desdemona. He has been sorely beaten tonight, Roderigo complains, but he fears that all he will get from his pain is the experience of it, a depleted purse, and not much more wisdom than he had before. Iago scolds the impatient suitor: everything takes time; wounds, for example, must heal by degrees. He reminds Roderigo that he works by wit, not witchcraft, and that wit must await the proper moment. He reviews the plan to Roderigo, pointing out that things are going as scheduled. Even though Roderigo has been slightly hurt in the action, Cassio has been dismissed. The rest will follow in good time, just as fruits must blossom before they can ripen. Be patient a little longer, Iago advises. Then, observing that the sun is rising, Iago remarks, "Pleasure and action make the hours seem short."

Dismissing Roderigo, Iago continues his cogitations. Two things must be done next, he decides: his wife, Emilia, must arrange a meeting between Cassio and Desdemona, and the Moor must be brought to witness their encounter.

Comment

Although the revenge-motive has initiated Iago's plot and continues as the basis of his action, Iago no longer contemplates the reasons for his malevolence. He is now totally immersed in the action of evil itself and observes how quickly time passes when one is engaged in "pleasure and action" (Contrast Iago's failure to mull over the cause for the revenge and his pleasure in evil action with Othello's concern for "the cause, the cause" even as he is about to slay Desdemona.) Iago's moves continues to be associated with diabolism. When he disclaims "villainy" or denies the use of witchcraft, he is suggesting his affiliation with both forms of evil.

SUMMARY

This scene accomplishes the following purposes:

1. The plot is advanced as Iago has a brilliant success in "sabotaging" Cassio, while keeping himself completely in the clear. In fact, he gains greater favor for his own claim to the lieutenancy and still manages to remain or friendly terms with Cassio, so that he can continue to abuse him.

2. Othello's character is amplified. His ability to punish a culprit even though he loves him deeply is

revealed in Othello's summary dismissal of Cassio and prepares us for his subsequent mistreatment of Desdemona. He continues to display his open and his trust in the appearances of men when he accepts Iago's grief-ridden face as a true show of grief and Iago's testimony as the whole truth of Cassio's disgraceful behavior.

3. Cassio's noble and trusting nature is demonstrated by his innocent faith in Iago and aligns him with Othello, a man of similar nature, who will also become a victim of Iago.

4. Iago's characterization becomes more and more dehumanized in this scene as Shakespeare probes into the nature of evil and associates Iago with "knavery," "villainy," the "Divinity of hell," "devils," and "witchcraft." Iago expresses his "pleasure" at the action of the night and displays the malicious glee at turning goodness to evil, which is commonly associated with demonic forces.

5. Roderigo continues his function as Iago's dupe and the impatient suitor of Desdemona. In this role, he urges Iago to new depths of deviltry and so assists in the movement of the plot.

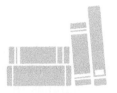

OTHELLO

ACT 3

. . . .

ACT III: SCENE 1

It is morning now. Cassio is seen in the court before the castle in the company of musicians whom he has engaged to play for Othello. He bids them play briefly, and when the General appears, they are to wish him "Good morrow."

As the musicians begin to blow their tune, a Clown emerges from the castle and asks them if their instruments have been to Naples.

Comment

This is apparently an **allusion** to the nasal drawl of Neopolitan speech, or to the nasality caused by venereal disease for which Naples was notorious.

The musicians identify their noise-makers as "wind instruments," which incites the Clown to several ribald puns on "wind," "tale," and "tail." The Clown delivers a gratuity from the General and tells them that he only admires music that cannot be heard. Unable to comply with this request, the musicians depart.

Comment

This comic interval, which opens the third act of the play, is devised to relieve and relax audience tensions which have been built up in the previous scene. It is also an attempt to favor the "groundlings" (vulgar members of the audience) with some ribald **burlesque**. The monstrous deeds of the night have been developed as far as they can go for the time being. Now in the light of day the musicians' pipes and the Clown's puns blow away the evils of the night. Since a minimum of scenery was used on the Elizabethan stage, intervals such as this one also set the time and place of the new action.

Cassio next addresses the Clown, and curbing his "quillets" (word-play) with a piece of gold, he asks him to entreat Emilia to have a word with him.

Iago arrives and is surprised to see Cassio stirring so early. Cassio informs the ancient that he has taken the liberty to send for Emilia in order to ask her to arrange an interview with Desdemona. Iago promises to send her down immediately and offers to assist further by drawing the Moor out of the way so that the interview can be held privately. As Iago leaves on his errand, Cassio remarks, "I never knew / A Florentine more kind and honest."

Comment

References to Iago's "honesty" run like a **refrain** throughout the play. Tragically ironic, these references serve as continual reminders, even in relatively innocent scenes such as this one, that all is not what it seems to be, that Iago is not "honest."

Emilia arrives promptly, greets the "good lieutenant," and expresses her sympathy for his misfortune. She informs Cassio that the General and his wife are discussing his misadventure at this very moment. Desdemona is already defending his cause, but the Moor has replied that Cassio's victim, Montano, is a very prominent man in Cyprus and has important connections. It would be bad policy to reinstate Cassio, Othello feels, even though he loves his former lieutenant dearly. In fact, Othello "needs no other suitor but his likings," and were it not for political prudence, he would reappoint Cassio at the first opportunity. Despite Emilia's report, Cassio importunes an interview with Desdemona, and Emilia agrees to arrange one.

Comment

Desdemona, we learn, is already inclined to assist Cassio. She has not seen him since her debarkation on the previous day, though perhaps momentarily during the night, but she has known him in Venice, as we learn later on. She believes he has given her husband loyal service. Othello's reasons for dismissing Cassio have been suggested before; they are now given emphasis through Emilia's restatement of them. Othello is, above all, a good governor, diplomatic and politic, and does not wish to arouse the hostility of the Cypriots.

SUMMARY

This scene accomplishes the following:

1. It effects a transition between Acts II and III, sets the time and place of the new action, and accomplishes comic relief from the tensions of the previous scene.

2. Cassio's impatience is displayed and advances the action of the plot. Although he learns from Emilia that the Moor has forgiven him, he is not content until he is completely restored. His impatience makes him arrange a meeting with Desdemona and provide Iago with the means of furthering his schemes.

ACT III: SCENE 2

This scene of less than ten lines takes place in a room in the Castle where Othello is conducting business with Iago and several gentlemen. Concluding his affairs, Othello hands over some letters to Iago which are to be given to one of the pilots of the fleet and delivered to Venice. He tells Iago he will be inspecting the "works" (fortifications) and asks the ancient to report to him there on his return. The gentlemen accompany Othello as he departs to make the inspection.

SUMMARY

This scene shows that Othello is engaged in business, thereby leaving Desdemona free to conduct her interview with Cassio. Iago has promised to keep him out of the way, but we shall soon see that he has no intention of doing so.

ACT III: SCENE 3

This scene of great length, almost 480 lines, is one of the greatest and most astounding in English literature. Dramatically, it is a technical achievement that has no match, for it aptly deals with psychological action rather than physical action, yet it does not allow audience interest to flag for a moment. Drama is basically an imitation of experience through action. It is easier to stage a physical conflict (and psychological changes directly resulting from such conflict) than to dramatize psychological persuasion and the process by which a character yields to this persuasion. Some terrible events occur during this scene, but they happen in the mind, in the psychological changes wrought in Othello by Iago's skillful manipulation of words and ideas. With the exception of strategic entrances and exits, there is relatively little physical movement in the scene. Nevertheless, it is full of inner action and is breathtaking in its intensity.

The third scene of Act III shifts to a garden in the castle where Desdemona, Cassio, and Emilia conduct the interview, which was originally suggested by Iago. Cassio implores Desdemona to take swift action in his behalf, for he fears that long delays and postponements may cause Othello to forget him. Desdemona promises to act at once. She will watch Othello and "tame" and "talk him out of patience." She assures Cassio that she will plead his cause as if it were her own, "for thy solicitor shall rather die / Than give thy cause away."

Comment

Desdemona will, indeed, die in Cassio's cause; this is another instance of Shakespeare's dramatic **irony**. During the interview, a number of polite exchanges occur in which Desdemona behaves just as Iago had predicted she would. She is bounteous in nature and certainly is easily subdued "in any honest suit."

Toward the end of the conversation, Othello and Iago are seen approaching. The forthright and uninhibited Desdemona bids him stay to hear her speak in his defense, but Cassio is too embarrassed to face the General he has offended and abruptly takes his leave of the ladies.

Comment

Accidental behavior on the part of the principals aids Iago's machinations from the start. Shakespeare makes it abundantly clear that Iago can improvise shrewdly, and Cassio's hasty departure gives Iago his next opportunity to implement his scheme for revenge.

When he sees Cassio leave Desdemona, Iago mutters, as if to himself, "Ha! I like not that." Believing Iago has addressed him, Othello inquires, "What doest thou say?" Assuming reluctance to speak, Iago replied, "Nothing, my lord; or if - I know not what." Casually, Othello turns to another subject, "Was not that Cassio parted from my wife?" Affecting surprise, Iago answers evasively, "Cassio, my lord? No sure, I cannot think it, / That he would steal away so guilty-like, / Seeing you coming."

Comment

Iago has injected his first shot of poison into Othello's bloodstream and exhibits his full technical skill in creating suspicion. Clearly, Cassio is leaving the company of Desdemona, but Iago's pretended denial and his description of the "guilty-like" figure causes Othello to interpret the scene from Iago's malevolent point of view. It is not suspicion yet but curiosity.

Now Desdemona greets Othello and her first words are about Cassio, who "languishes in your displeasure." She pleads for "present reconciliation" between Othello and Cassio, for the latter has "erred in ignorance and not in cunning." But Othello, still curious to identify the "guilty-like" figure, wants to know if Cassio has just departed. He has, Desdemona replies, adding that Cassio has been humbled by grief and urging that Othello call him back at once.

Othello wants to postpone his forgiveness. (He is probably hoping that Cassio's misconduct will be forgotten presently, and the reinstatement can then be made without raising the objections of the entire town.) Desdemona, however, becomes insistent. In fact, she nags. She wonders what Othello would ask her to do that she would deny "or stand so mammering on." She reminds him how Cassio came wooing with him and defended him when Desdemona had disdained him. Finally, Othello yields, saying that he will deny her nothing. He beseeches her, in return, to leave him alone. Whereupon, Desdemona grants his wish immediately, calling upon Emilia to witness what an obedient wife she is. Upon her departure, Othello remarks: "Perdition catch my soul / But I do love thee! and when I love thee not, / Chaos is come again."

Comment

Another note of tragic **irony** and dramatic **foreshadowing** is present in Othello's last lines. When he finally does turn against his beloved wife, chaos does have a bloody reign.

Desdemona, in her ardent petition for Michael Cassio's cause, has reminded Othello about their close friendship. Cassio had helped him woo her, acting as a go-between for the lovers, in accordance with Renaissance romance tradition. Ever on the alert, Iago next takes up this point.

Iago asks Othello whether Cassio knew of his love when he first wooed Desdemona. Told that he did, Iago affects surprise at learning this. "Indeed," he exclaims and refuses to explain his surprise. He claims the question was asked only "for a satisfaction of my thought," and when probed for further explanation, he evasively parrots Othello's words:

Iago: I did not think he had been acquainted with her. Othello: O, yes, and went between us very oft. Iago: Indeed? Othello: Indeed? Ay, indeed! Discernst thou aught in that? Is he not honest? Iago: Honest, my lord? Othello: Honest? Ay, honest. Iago: My lord, for aught I know. Othello: What dost thou think? Iago: Think, my lord? Othello: Think, my lord? By heaven, he echoes me. . . .

Comment

Shakespeare creates a marvelous dramatic dialogue to show how suspicion can be created by insinuation and be left to feed and grow upon itself. The secret lies in avoiding explicit accusation. If a man says, "John stole five dollars," the accusation is both definite and limited. But if he says, "I didn't think you knew John," he immediately raises the question, "Why, what's the matter with John?" In the latter case, the insinuation is unlimited. The inquirer is encouraged to supply his own answers, and he is free to think the worst if he wishes to. This is Iago's technique: he fosters suspicion by using undefined insinuation.

Othello declares that Iago is playing echo "as if there were some monster in his thought / Too hideous to be shown."

Comment

Unconscious **irony**, such as Othello's **allusion** to "monstrous thoughts," permeates the play. It combines a touch of humor with tragic reminders and adds the element of horror to the events by associating them with "monstrousness" and at time with hell.

His curiosity excited, Othello appeals to Iago's love for him to reveal his thoughts. Iago answers this appeal indirectly. He asks if Othello is assured in his love for him; to which Othello replies he is convinced that Iago loves him. He adds that the delaying tactics Iago is using are tricks commonly employed by false, disloyal knaves. In "honest" Iago, however, these evasions indicate that Iago is a man who weighs his words carefully before speaking.

Thus assured, Iago states that he thinks Cassio is honest, and Othello agrees. Slyly, Iago next suggests that he has no basis for his belief in Cassio's honesty except the fact that "men should be what they seem." Infected by the suspicions Iago has successfully planted so quickly, Othello demands that Iago speak what he thinks no matter how horrible his thoughts may be. With a sense of timing and pace, Iago refuses to utter his thoughts at first. He pretends to be uncertain about his ideas. Suppose they are "vile and false"; after all, the best of men is subject to an occasional unclean thought. In a long, carefully measured preamble which says nothing definite, Iago points out his own tendency "to spy into abuses"; often his "jealousy" (suspicion) "shapes faults that are not." He cautions Othello against prying into his thoughts, for they are "not for your quiet nor your good." (This is the truth, of course, but Othello has no way of knowing that Iago is speaking with conscious irony.) Then, his famous speech on reputation in which he reverses the position he took when discussing the subject with Cassio (in II.iii), Iago asserts:

Who steals my purse steals trash; 'tis something, nothing; 'Twas mine, 'tis his, and has been slave to thousands; But he that filches from me my good name Robs me of that which not enriches him And makes me poor indeed.

Comment

When Iago asserts that "men should be what they seem," he makes another insinuation about Cassio and introduces the **theme** of appearance versus reality, which is reiterated throughout the play. The **theme** is brought into focus at this point for particular ironic purposes, but it also serves to create an atmosphere of universal doubt.

When Iago alludes to his own "jealousy," to his tendency to be "vicious in my guess," he increases Othello's suspense, while he creates, at the same time, an avenue of escape for himself, should Othello reject his suspicions.

Finally, Othello demands, "By heaven, I'll know thy thoughts." But Iago, adopting an air of rugged independence and injured integrity, replies firmly, "You cannot . . . / Nor shall not." "Ha!" cries Othello. This "Ha!" is open to two interpretations. One is that the image of Desdemona's infidelity has sprung into the mind of Othello. Iago has been able, by subtle insinuation, to bring it to a monstrous birth. The other interpretation is that the "Ha!" merely expresses Othello's impatience with Iago's reluctance to be straightforward. In an case, Iago now assumes that suspicion has taken hold of Othello and warns, "O, beware, my lord, of jealousy! / It is the green ey'd monster." Othello still fails to catch the drift of Iago's meaning. Is Iago trying to advise his master against a jealousy which he does not feel? Does Iago think that "blown surmises" and "inference" will make him jealous? Othello asks. Desdemona's behavior cannot be misinterpreted; though she is fair, enjoys feasts, loves company, has all the graces of speech, song, play, and dance, yet she is virtuous. Confidently, Othello states, "She had eyes, and chose me. No, Iago; / I'll see before I doubt." Furthermore, if he were ever furnished with proof, still he would not be jealous, for he would discard love and jealousy simultaneously.

Comment

As Desdemona tells Emilia in a later scene, Othello is not the jealous type. Othello believes this to be true himself. He is a confident man, assured in his own virtue and in his wife's, but he is curious. We have seen how his gorge began to rise when witnesses had refused to testify about Cassio's fight with Montano; we have seen him again cajoling, demanding, insisting on knowing the meaning of Iago's insinuations. It is this curiosity, not an inherently jealous or suspicious nature, which will cause

Othello to follow Iago's next piece of advice and seek out the truth of Iago's innuendoes.

Iago expresses pleasure at learning that Othello is not a jealous man, for this will give him leave to prove his loyalty with "franker spirit." At the moment he has no proof, but he suggests that Othello keep his eye on Desdemona and Cassio. He informs Othello that he knows the ways of Venetian women very well. Their conscience on matters of adultery "is not to leave it undone, but keep't unknown." He reminds Othello of Desdemona's former duplicities: she deceived her father by marrying the Moor, and when she pretended to fear Othello's looks, she loved them most.

Comment

It should be remembered that Iago and Desdemona are Venetian, while Othello is a Moor, who has spent most of his life at war and in strange, uncivilized lands. He does not know the ways of Venice, nor of its women, and Iago's information is curious and interesting to him. He is completely unaware of the fact that Desdemona's pretended disdain was part of the pattern of courtship in Venice.

Having gone as far as the situation will permit, Iago now apologizes for imparting his suspicions to the General. Othello protests that he is deeply indebted to Iago for unburdening his thoughts. He insists they have not troubled him, as Iago continues to apologize for expressing such unsettling thoughts and as he cautions the Moor not to misunderstand him. Iago has only expressed his suspicions, nothing more. This is understood, Othello claims, "And yet, how nature erring from itself - "

Comment

Iago has indeed struck home. At the very same time that the Moor insists that he is not moved to jealousy, his mind begins to inquire, "And yet. . . ." The seed of suspicion has been sown.

Seizing on the idea of "erring nature" in Othello's moment of doubt, Iago pounces, "Ay, there's the point!" He submits that "her" (Desdemona's) unwillingness to accept the numerous matches her father proposed to her with men of similar "clime, complexion, and degree" (which it was natural for her to do) marks her as a woman with "a will most rank," in which "foul disproportion, thoughts unnatural" are harbored. With all due apologies to Othello, Iago adds, he is not speaking of Desdemona in particular.

Even so, Iago fears, "her" will, on reconsideration, may cause her to compare Othello with her own countrymen and to repent her original choice of husband. Othello has heard enough. He bids Iago farewell, asking him to report if he perceives anything more and to set his wife Emilia to observe Desdemona.

As soon as Iago leaves, Othello gives vent to the grief that has been building up. "Why did I marry," he groans. He is certain that Iago knows more than he is willing to tell.

Comment

We have now reached the **climax** - the highest point of tension, the decisive turning point-of the play. And what a **climax** it is! Exclusively mental, the scene is written with superb dramatic artistry. A thought is born in Othello's mind; the monstrous image of Desdemona's infidelity is conjured up. Dramatically, this hideous, most painful thought is indicated by a single cry of painful awareness, by the pathos of the simple ejaculation, "Why did I marry?"

Iago's consummate skill in innuendo has sired the "green-ey'd monster"; Othello's imagination will nurture it. Iago has said nothing definite; he has, in fact, warned Othello against Iago's own suspicious nature, his tendency to think the worst, his possible inaccuracy; and Othello has fallen heedlessly into the trap.

Suspicion, as well as jealousy itself, is an important **theme** in Othello's tragedy. Shakespeare shows how suspicion is sown and how easily it feeds upon itself. Frank communication is the only cure for it, but suspicion makes communication difficult from the start. Perhaps, Othello's love for Desdemona is imperfect, is tainted with egoism or insecurity, for he seems to fall into the trap too readily. Yet, he has every reason to believe "honest and loyal" Iago even though Iago has only voiced suspicions without proof.

Iago returns with an afterthought. Making another plea for moderation, he suggests that Cassio should not have his place back yet, so that Othello can be watchful and note whether or not Desdemona goes out of her way to support him. With that Iago takes his leave once more.

A soliloquy of Othello's fellows; it is indignant and pathetic at the same time. Iago, he thinks, is "exceeding honest" and really knows what life is about. He himself is a black man, on the older side ("declin'd / Into the vale of years") and has not the gift of making sweet love-talk as "chamberers" (wanton gallants) do.

Comment

The fact that Othello is "declin'd into . . . years" may have special significance in his characterization. The critic Granville-Barker explains that in all Othello's years he has never been in love. Late in his life, he meets Desdemona, whose love for him creates a new "self" in Othello. "It is a self created by her love for him," Granville-Barker states, "and will be the more dependent, therefore, upon his faith in that. It will be besides, a dangerously defenseless self, since he is no longer a young man . . . and between it and the rest of this character, fully formed and set in far other molds, there can be no easy interplay. The division between old and new in him-between seasoned soldier and enraptured bride-groom-presages the terrible cleavage to come."

Some unpleasant images of life with an unfaithful wife pass ominously through Othello's mind. Then, as he sees her coming, the nightmare lifts and gives way to the heavenly image of Desdemona: "If she be false, O, then heaven mocks itself! / I'll not believe it."

But the psychological stress to which Iago has submitted him now has its physical effects. Faintly, he accuses himself of harboring evil thoughts. Then Othello attributes him mutterings to a severe headache. Desdemona offers him a handkerchief (later we find that it is a special heirloom) with which to bind his forehead. In his agitation, Othello drops it, and it is retrieved by Emilia, who recalls that Iago has tried to persuade her to steal it for quite some time. Now that she has the opportunity, she decides to have the "work" (embroidered design) copied and given to Iago, though she has no idea what he wants it for. But then Iago enters and forcibly takes it from her, refusing to return it, although Emilia complains that Desdemona, "Poor lady, she'll run mad / When she shall lack it." Iago summarily orders Emilia away.

Left alone, Iago works on his plot again. He will plant the handkerchief in Cassio's lodging. Something may come of it. The Moor is already inclined toward suspicion, and Iago is sure it will soon grow into a belief.

Comment

There has been much adverse criticism of the plot machinery of "the dropped handkerchief," dating as far back as Thomas Rymer, who in *Short View of Tragedy* (1693) dismissed Othello as the "bloody tragical farce of the dropped handkerchief." Even the modern critic E. E. Stoll is disturbed by the handkerchief device: "The numerous coincidences (like Othello's and Desdemona's not noticing that the precious handkerchief is the one that she had dropped, and Bianca's arrival, in Act IV, i, precisely when wanted) may, by rapidity of action, be obscured but not justified-unless they are in melodrama."

In several sad, melodious lines, uttered like an incantation, Iago observes the approaching figure of Othello:

.... Not poppy, nor madragora, Nor all the drowsy syrups of the world, Shall ever medicine thee to that sweet sleep Which thou ow'dst yesterday.

Othello greets Iago with the violent accusation: "Ha! Ha! false to me?"

Comment

For a moment, it may be believed that Othello has come to his senses, has uncovered Iago's deception, and is about to tear him limb from limb as he soon threatens to do. Through the use of ambiguous lines, Shakespeare creates momentary suspense, but the anticipation of Iago's discovery is shortly reversed.

George Lyman Kittredge, the famous Shakespearean scholar, interpreted this line as a reflective one. Othello does not see Iago, and he is talking of Desdemona, whom he addresses in his mind as false. In view of what follows this need not be the case.

Othello finds Iago false because he has set Othello "on the rack" by giving him "to know't a little," that is, by causing him to suspect his wife without proving the case finally, one way or the other. We have seen the rage which curiosity awakens in Othello on several other occasions. He cannot abide ignorance of a situation or doubt about the nature of events; he himself recognizes what agony it is to him to know only a little. Not long before (11. 241-2 of the same scene), Othello voices his suspicion of Iago's concealments: "This honest creature doubtless / Sees and knows more, much more, than he unfolds." Now he calls Iago "false" for setting him in doubt and for continuing to withhold information from him.

When Iago inquires the reason for Othello's wrath, Othello replies that before Iago had given him reason to suspect Desdemona, Othello had enjoyed her company freely. Now his pleasures are tainted by doubt. Hitherto, Othello says, "I found not Cassio's kisses on her lips." If only he knew nothing at all, Othello complains. Othello is deeply depressed. Empassioned by despair, Othello bids farewell to "Pride, pomp, and circumstance of glorious war." Finally, he turns against Iago again: "Villain, be sure thou prove my love a whore!" (For once, Othello has correctly identified the character of "honest" Iago, but, ironically, he does not know it.) He demands that Iago bring him "ocular proof" of Desdemona's treachery. If Iago has lied, he will wish he had been born a dog rather than answer to Othello's "wak'd wrath."

Owing to his lack of self-control, the result of his tortured state of mind, Othello is here no match for the calculated hypocrisy of Iago. Iago answers Othello's demands with a complaint to the world at large. After all, what has he done but be "honest" and demonstrate his love for Othello? "Take note, take note, O world," Iago cried, "To be direct and honest is not safe."

(There is grim humor in Iago's complaint, for we know that he means exactly what he is saying. Since Othello does not, this is another instance of dramatic irony.) Othello recants his threat; Iago must continue to be honest. By way of apology, Othello explains his agonizing conflict: "I think my wife be honest, and think she is not." He describes his new hateful image of Desdemona; her face is "now begrim'd and black as my own face." Othello now changes his threat to a humble request for satisfaction; then, his determination returning, he asserts that he will be satisfied. (Othello has played right into Iago's hands; the villain has a handkerchief, we may recall.) "But how? how satisfied, my lord?" Iago asks. Do you want to see the actual act of adultery being committed? This would be hard to bring about, but "imputation and strong circumstances" are easily produced. Othello bites. "Give a living reason she's disloyal," he asks Iago. Now Iago tells how he has recently slept in the same bed with Cassio and has heard him mutter various compromising things about Desdemona in his sleep. Othello reacts violently to this tale: "O monstrous! monstrous!"

Comment

Shakespeare makes it clear that Othello's capacity for judgment has deteriorated; Othello is prepared to accept less in the way of solid evidence than he was initially. Reason is less able to guide him as his passion takes over, and he has increasing difficulty in distinguishing between reality and appearance. This scene has already marked Othello's willingness to believe the suspicions Iago has been feeding him. Now, with his cry of "monstrous," Othello shows that he is utterly convinced. The "monstrous birth" that Iago had planned at the end of Act I has been labored forth. The **climax** of the play having been reached, the resolution - the working out of the plot which has been developed up to this point - begins.

Affecting moderation, Iago says, "Nay, this was but a dream." (He has something more tangible to offer.) Iago now introduces the matter of the handkerchief "spotted with strawberries," which, luckily, he has acquired only a few moments ago. Cleverly improvising, Iago claims that he has seen Cassio wipe his beard with it. (Apparently, Othello has not noticed that it was this same handkerchief which Desdemona had offered him for binding his forehead.) Iago declares that "it speaks against her with other proofs." Utterly convinced for this moment Othello completely loses control: "All my fond love thus do I blow to heaven . . . / Arise, black vengeance, from the hollow hell! Agitated by his terrible passion, he is reduced to calling for "blood, blood, blood," as Iago prods him to further depths by urging patience, and by suggesting that he may change his mind.

In the heat of anger, Othello swears never to change his mind and, like the icy currents of the Pontic sea, never to change his course, never to look back, never to cease till he has had his revenge. Kneeling, he takes a sacred vow on these words. Iago kneels beside the crazed Moor and adds his own oath, swearing to serve the wronged Othello in "what bloody business ever."

Comment

The diabolical oath which Othello and Iago make in terms of "blood, blood, blood," "bloody thought," and "what bloody business ever," has frequently been compared with a devil's compact, sealed (as Doctor Faustus' was) by the sign of blood.

Othello accepts Iago's fellowship in revenge and consigns Cassio to Iago's sword. Iago now agrees to exchange Cassio's friendship for the Moor's, but he sustains his role as "honest" Iago by asking that Desdemona be spared. Passionately, Othello denies this request, damning Desdemona as a "lewd minx." He retires to devise a means of killing her, but not before appointing Iago his new lieutenant.

SUMMARY

It is not easy to summarize this lengthy but fast-moving scene. Every word and gesture has had special meaning in drawing the play to its **climax**. Iago is like a deadly insect gradually stalking, then stinging its victim to death; each of his moves, whether calculated or improvised, is perfectly timed.

1. The scene is designed to convince us through dramatic representation that a man like Iago can deceive a man like Othello and lead him to a

dangerous and destructive resolution. Therefore, from start to finish, the scene demonstrates Iago's powers of psychological and verbal manipulation. Shakespeare achieves his design superbly.

2. Iago manipulates Othello so that the poisoned thought of Desdemona's adultery springs directly from the mind of Othello, although the venom has been injected by Iago. Iago has given this scene its potent atmosphere, but the fact that Othello seems to have thought of the idea himself gives it a more corrosive effect.

3. The scene shows Othello in a state of mental flux. The state of his mind changes in response to each of Iago's proddings. Othello becomes curious, then insistent, then enraged. His doubt subsides temporarily when he sees the heavenly Desdemona again. But doubt, once planted, burgeons rapidly. Othello is completely consumed by it and is prepared to take Iago's allegations concerning Cassio's dream and Desdemona's handkerchief as evidence itself.

4. This is the climactic scene of the play, beginning with the insinuations about the "guilty-like" Cassio and ending with Othello's oath of revenge.

5. The beginning of Othello's moral decline is portrayed in this scene. From the moment he allows Iago's insinuations to take hold of his mind, the fiber of his character begins to disintegrate.

ACT III: SCENE 4

The scene takes place in front of the castle. Accompanied by Emilia, Desdemona asks the Clown where Cassio "lies" (1. lodges, dwells; 2. speaks falsely, "stabs"). The Clown replies equivocally with puns on "lie," "stab," and "lodge." He fails to produce the information, for he really does not know. In periphrastic terms of a comic nature, the Clown agrees, however, to search out Cassio.

Comment

The Clown, a stock character in Shakespearean drama, appears infrequently and briefly in Othello. Both here and in III.i, the Clown is used to provide comic relief, following a terrific scene of dark passion. As one critic describes him, Othello "in commotion reminds us rather of the fury of the elements than of the tumult of common human passion." After the emotional hurricane of the preceding scene, the Clown's puns are as welcome as the calm following a storm.

Desdemona tells Emilia that she is disturbed by the loss of her handkerchief; she would rather lose a purse full of money. But she consoles herself (with the dramatically ironic), "And but my noble Moor / Is true of mind and made of no such baseness / As jealous creatures are, it were enough / To put him to ill thinking." (Attention is called here to the importance of the handkerchief in the plot and to Othello's usually unsuspecting nature. Desdemona will be unable to recognize Othello's jealousy when she sees it, for she has a decidedly different view of his character.) Surprised that a wife can so describe her husband, Emilia inquires, "Is Othello not jealous?" Emphatically,

Desdemona replies, "I think the sun where he was born / Drew all such humors from him."

Comment

Emilia's experience as Iago's wife makes her think on principle that all men are jealous. She does not know about Othello's suspicions or for what purpose the handkerchief has been used.

Othello enters and takes Desdemona's hand. Dissembling affection, he says her hand is moist. Desdemona interprets "moist" to mean that she has not been dried by age and sorrow, but Othello says that it is a sign of "fruitfulness and a liberal heart" (wantonness is suggested). In pretended jest, he prescribes loss of liberty, fasting, and prayer as a remedy for the "sweating devil" (sprit of sexual desire), which he finds in her hand. It is a noble hand, Othello continues, and a "frank" one. Desdemona replies that her hand is indeed a "frank" one (meaning "generous," magnanimous"), for it was this hand that gave her heart to Othello.

Comment

In medieval physiology, the body contained four major fluids or "humors": blood, yellow bile, phlegm, and spleen (black bile or black choler). The preponderance of a particular fluid in a person marked him as sanguine, choleric, phlegmatic, or splenetic (melancholic). It was believed that the mental disposition of a person corresponded to his physiological attributes. The heat and moisture, which Othello mentions, were characteristics of the sanguine temperament, which was a cheerful, generous, amorous one. Othello stresses the amorous (lecherous) aspect of Desdemona's nature, while Desdemona emphasized her love and generosity.

Following this mingled conversation in which Desdemona playfully reverses Othello's insinuating diagnosis, Desdemona informs her husband that she has sent for Cassio to speak to Othello. Othello ignores this piece of information and, claiming a cold in the head, asks for her handkerchief. Desdemona expresses regret that she does not have it with her. Othello reproves her for not having it and then gives an account of why the handkerchief is so important. Since the handkerchief plays so important a part in the plot machinery of the play, the description is repeated here.

That handkerchief Did an Egyptian to my mother give. She was a charmer, and could almost read The thoughts of people. She told her, while she kept it, 'T would make her amiable and subdue my father Entirely to her love; but if she lost it Or made a gift of it, my father's eye Should hold her loathly, and his spirits should hunt After new fancies. She, dying, gave it me, And bid me, when my fate would have me wive, To give it her. I did so; and take heed ont'; Make it a darling like your precious eye. To lose't or give't away were such perdition As nothing else could match.

"There's magic in the web of it," Othello assures the distressed wife. It was sewn by a two-hundred year old Sybil in "prophetic fury" and "dy'd in mummy which the skillful / Conserv'd of maiden's hearts."

Comment

The handkerchief was the Moor's first gift to Desdemona. Emilia refers to it as "that the Moor first gave to Desdemona" (III.

iii.309), and Othello tells Iago "'twas my first gift" (III.iii.436). If this gift was given during the courtship and is truly a magic handkerchief, then Othello did use magic to win Desdemona, and he lied to the Duke's court. If the courtship was conducted without magic as Othello told the court, he may be lying now; the handkerchief may not have these properties. Othello may be inventing the tale to test or frighten Desdemona. On the other hand, the handkerchief may have been the first gift after marriage, none having been given before; Othello's present story then may be taken as a true one. The problem is a complex one, for Othello had an open nature when he testified in the Venetian court; now, under Iago's influence, he is capable of duplicity. The commentaries which follow are based on the assumptions that the handkerchief was a marriage gift and contained magic properties.

Desdemona's surprise and distress mount as she listens to this tale. She cannot produce the handkerchief, but she denies that it is lost. (This is Desdemona's first deception, and, as we shall see, it will contribute to her ultimate destruction.) Artfully, she refuses to fetch the handkerchief, claiming that Othello has used the story as a trick to dissuade her from discussing Cassio.

Comment

By providing it with a history, Shakespeare emphasizes the significance of the handkerchief and prevents it from becoming a trivial prop. The magic origins of the handkerchief make it symbolic of Othello's mysterious and romantic past, which originally had won Desdemona's love. It is also symbolic of constancy in love, one of the important **themes** of the play. By losing the handkerchief, Desdemona symbolically loses Othello's love. Thus, the handkerchief becomes more than a cog in the machinery of melodrama; the tale of its magic properties makes it an organic element in the texture of the play.

Repeatedly, Othello insists on seeing the handkerchief, while Desdemona answers each of his demands with a plea for Cassio. Othello leaves in a rage.

Comment

Once more Othello becomes enraged when his demands are refused. This time his anger is far more ominous, for he utters no threats. During his earlier inquiries into Cassio's misconduct and Iago's suspicions, he relied on Iago's word. His dependence for information on his newly-appointed lieutenant increases. He will turn to Iago again and believe what he is told, for Othello must have prompt answers to his question.

As Othello departs, Emilia repeats the question she had asked prior to this angry interview, "Is not this man jealous?" (This time, however, the question is rhetorical.) Desdemona confesses, "I ne'er saw this before." (His wife is the first to note that Othello has changed.) She repeats her concern for the lost handkerchief, but Emilia, still wondering over Othello's strange behavior, merely reflects on the fickleness of men, "They eat us hungrily, and when they are full, / They belch us."

Comment

The plot thickens. Emilia does not say what has happened to the handkerchief, though she knows perfectly well (III.iii). Like her cynical husband, she believes in the worst generalities that can be made of man. To her way of thinking, the handkerchief is irrelevant; she is convinced that Othello has tired of his wife and is using the lost handkerchief as an excuse to berate her.

Iago and Cassio now join the ladies. Iago has been insisting that Cassio importune Desdemona once more. Cassio asks Desdemona for a final decision; he does not want to keep pleading. If his reinstatement is denied, he will seek some other fortune. Regretfully, Desdemona explains her situation. She has been pressing his suit, but Othello is not in a good mood, his "humor" has altered. In reply to Iago's question, Emilia says that Othello hat just gone away "in strange unquietness." Iago pretends to be surprised at the news. He has seen Othello maintain his calm in the fiercest heat of battle, even when his brother's life was destroyed. "Something of moment" must be disturbing the Moor. Desdemona urges Iago to see Othello.

Comment

By suggesting that "something of moment" is afoot, Iago hopes to keep Desdemona from guessing that Othello is jealous. By maintaining her ignorance, he can continue to use her innocent association with Cassio to his own advantage.

Meanwhile, Iago's facts about Othello's life and character heighten the contrast between Othello's "strange" new humor and his previous one. Desdemona's statement that Othello is "in humor alter'd," suggests that Othello is now suffering from too much spleen (melancholy), whereas previously he had been phlegmatic (cool, self-possessed, slow to anger), as Iago describes the Moor on the battlefield.

Shakespeare's art is a subtle one. Othello is central to the play, and even when he does not appear, his characterization is continued. The single reference to his "alter'd humor" and Iago's subsequent description of Othello in battle achieve two purposes: in terms of the plot, Desdemona is misled to believe that Othello suffers under cares of state; in terms of the character, Othello's change is observed and emphasized.

Latching on to Iago's suggestions that something important is disturbing her husband, the humble Desdemona decides it is some business with Venice or some matter of state. Apologizing for her husband, Desdemona explains to Emilia that men frequently mistreat their wives when they have great worries on their minds. "We must not think men are gods," she cautions Emilia, blaming herself for thinking unkindly of Othello before Iago's suggestion clarified his outrageous behavior. Emilia, more realistic, prays to heaven that state-matters are truly the cause of Othello's conduct, and not some jealousy of Desdemona. Thinking of her own husband, Emilia asserts that wives need not give their husbands cause for jealousy, for "'tis a monster / Begot upon itself, born on itself."

Comment

In her description of jealousy, Emilia echoes Iago, who called jealousy "a green-ey'd monster which doth mock / The meat it feeds on." Emilia's knowledge of jealous men has been learned at Iago's school, which Othello has been attending too. Her interpretation of Othello's behavior is the correct one, of course.

Despite her awareness of Othello's ill-humor, Desdemona decides to find him and once more advance Cassio's cause, this time "to my uttermost." Cassio is asked to await her return.

As Desdemona and Emilia leave, Cassio is left alone onstage. Bianca arrives and is greeted with much familiarity by Cassio, who states that he was planning to pay her a visit very shortly. Bianca too was just on her way to Cassio's lodgings, for, she complains, he has not been to see her for an entire week. This is a long time for lovers. Cassio explains that his absence was owing to the pressure of "leaden thoughts," but he promises to make up for his absence when he can do so without interruption. As if to turn the conversation, Cassio gives Bianca a handkerchief and asks her to copy its pattern. Bianca is immediately suspicious that the handkerchief has come from some new mistress. Cassio explains that he found it in his chamber and does not know its owner. Before he must return it, he would like to have a copy of the design, which he finds most attractive.

Comment

The embroidered design of the handkerchief spotted with strawberries was sewn by a Sybil in "prophetic fury." Apparently, it has the magic power of winning the admiration of those who see it. Desdemona had a special affinity for this token from her husband even before she heard its history. Iago too had liked the design and had often urged Emilia to steal the handkerchief for him. Perhaps, he intended even then to use it in some plot; perhaps, he was drawn to it by its magic powers.

The chain of accidents connected with the handkerchief strains credibility if the magic cloth is viewed as an ordinary accessory. The Elizabethan audience was a susceptible one, and many of its members believed in magic. (Witches were burned in Salem long after Shakespeare's day.) It would be better to suspend one's disbelief in magic than to allow modern reason to spoil Shakespeare's play.

Cassio asks Bianca to leave him, for he is awaiting the General and does not want to be found with a woman. Bianca is reluctant to go; she asks Cassio to walk her a bit of the way and presses him to dine with her that night. Anxious to get rid of her, Cassio promises to see her soon, and Bianca takes her leave as the scene ends.

SUMMARY

This scene is important in several respects.

1. It establishes the fact that Othello's character is undergoing change. Hitherto self-possessed and slow to anger, he is rapidly becoming irritable, strangely unquiet, and melancholic. He is clearly struggling with his jealousy and attempts to check Iago's allegations in regard to the handkerchief. For the first time in the play, "open-natured" Othello practices duplicity by confronting his wife indirectly and making evil insinuations about her character under the guise of good fellowship.

2. The plot progresses slowly as the implications of the dropped handkerchief are examined in detail from various points of view. Its strange history is unfolded, giving it symbolic value in the development of the theme of constancy; Othello makes the handkerchief vital to his love for Desdemona; Desdemona's distress over the loss of it increases; Emilia is unimpressed with the importance of the handkerchief; Cassio's innocent admiration of its design arouses Bianca's jealousy, and his own interest in it portends doom for its owner, Desdemona.

3. The scene reveals that minor moral weaknesses are widespread (and implies that minor vices lead to major catastrophes). Desdemona lies directly (about the loss of the handkerchief); Emilia lies indirectly (by withholding information about it); and Cassio arranges an assignation with a woman of loose morals. All these acts play their parts in the final catastrophe.

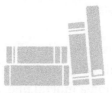

OTHELLO

ACT 4

. . . .

ACT IV: SCENE 1

The scene is again the yard before the Castle. Iago and Othello are in the midst of an earnest conversation. (Their opening remarks are somewhat ambiguous, but they may be interpreted in terms of the lines which follow.) Iago asks Othello if he will think a kiss in private an "unauthoriz'd" (unwarrantable) thing, and Othello insists that he does not think but knows it to be so. Next, Iago asks if it is possible for Desdemona to spend an hour in bed with a lover and mean no harm. Othello, of course, asserts that this is impossible. Iago contends that as long as they do nothing, they are merely committing a minor sin, "But if I give my wife a handkerchief - "

Comment

Iago is engaged in the game of insinuation again. He states that lying in bed naked so long as one does nothing is only a minor sin, but if one gives his wife a handkerchief - The unfinished sentence implies the following ending: if she gives it to another man, then the sin is major, a mortal one, an unpardonable one.

Reminded of the handkerchief, Othello compares it to a "raven o'er the infected house." Iago pretends to make light of the handkerchief (implying that he has more incriminating evidence to report). Cassio has admitted his intimacies with Desdemona. Othello is thoroughly shaken. His mind gives way, and he utters a series of disjointed and confused thoughts (all highly relevant to the situation, but without **syntax**) before falling into a trance. Chanting diabolically, Iago gloats, "Work on / My medicine, work! Thus credulous fools are caught."

Cassio enters at this point. In reply to his question, Iago states that the Moor has "fall'n into an epilepsy." Refusing his assistance, Iago asks Cassio to withdraw, promising to speak to him after the General recovers. Cassio leaves.

As soon as Othello recovers. Iago asks about his head. Othello imagines he is being mocked (that an **allusion** has been made to the horns on his head, traditionally ascribed to cuckolded husbands). Iago denies having made such an **allusion**. He wishes Othello would behave like a man, or, if he feels like a beast (with cuckold's horns), then he should be comforted in the knowledge that the city is full of such beasts. In fact, Othello is better off than millions of men who do not know they are being deceived. No, Iago asserts, he personally would rather know the truth about his wife, and knowing his own nature (vengeful), he knows what she would be (punished). Othello is impressed by Iago's wisdom.

Next, Iago informs Othello that Cassio had been there and that he will come back. Othello is to conceal himself, and he will overhear the truth from Cassio's own lips. Othello hides.

Comment

Once before Iago had suggested that Othello hide, but Othello, then direct and open-natured, had refused to do so. Brabantio was on his way to have the Moor arrested, and the Moor insisted on being found. Othello's willingness to hide at Iago's urging bears witness to the deterioration of his character.

Cassio returns, and Iago begins to question him not about Desdemona, as Othello has been led to believe, but about Bianca, the local prostitute.

Iago starts a stream of rough banter, alleging, among other things, that Bianca has spread the rumor that Cassio intends to marry her. Cassio thinks this is a hilarious joke. Meanwhile, Othello in his hiding place interprets the laughter as Cassio's exultation over his conquest. Bianca returns at this point and angrily shakes Desdemona's handkerchief in Cassio's face. On second thought, she has decided that Cassio has been unfaithful to her, that the handkerchief is "some minx's token," and that she would be a fool to "take out" (copy) its work. When Bianca leaves in a huff, Iago sends Cassio after her to quiet her down, learning first that Cassio will dine at Bianca's that night. Othello comes out of hiding prepared to murder his former officer.

Comment

This scene indicates that Othello is attempting a real investigation, but he is too much blinded by jealousy to understand what he sees and to realize that he cannot really hear the conversation between Iago and Cassio.

Othello claims his heart has turned to stone, yet when he thinks of Desdemona's sweetness, her skill in embroidery, in music, her plenteous wit and invention, he is deeply moved, "But yet the pity of it, Iago! O Iago, the pity of it, Iago!"

Comment

Although Desdemona's virtues have been extolled before, Othello's description suggests that she is a "perfect lady" of the sort outlined in Castiglione's Book of the Courtier. Being unbookish and untutored in the ways of Venetian society, Othello does not realize that Desdemona cannot be the adulteress he thinks. This is indeed a pity.

Othello is now totally convinced of Desdemona's guilt. Determined to kill her, he asks Iago to get him poison. But Iago suggests a more symbolic revenge: "Strangle her in . . .the bed she hath contaminated." Othello is pleased with the justice of this method. Iago undertakes to dispose of Cassio.

A trumpet sounds. Desdemona enters in the company of her cousin Lodovico, the Venetian ambassador, and other attendants. As Othello reads the letter he has received from Venice, Desdemona explains to Lodovico that there has been a misunderstanding between Othello and Cassio, in which she hopes her cousin will clear up. Othello listens to her conversation, interjecting ominous remarks, which he pretends are commentaries on the letter. Angered by Desdemona's reference to "the love I bear to Cassio," Othello asks her if she is wise (that is, to admit her love publicly). When she expresses her pleasure at Cassio's appointment as Othello's deputy-governor, he becomes violently angry and publicly strikes her.

Everyone in the distinguished assembly is shocked. Othello's private torture is now public property. He deepens the effect of his barbarous conduct by hinting at her promiscuity: "Sir, she can turn, and turn, and yet go on / And turn again." Lodovico can make no sense of the behavior of the "noble Moor," the man of undaunted courage and monumental dignity, whom he had hitherto known.

After Othello storms out, Iago insinuates that Othello is often brutal and could get worse. But after arousing Lodovico's curiosity, he puritanically asserts: "It is not honesty in me to speak / What I have seen and known." The innuendo strikes home at once. Urged to observe the Moor himself, Lodovico departs, convinced that he has been "deceived in him [Othello]."

SUMMARY

This scene continues to portray the debasement of Othello, deepening our sense of pity for the utter disintegration of the noble character. The audience's hatred for Iago is intensified as pity for Othello increases. The scene shows the following things:

1. Othello has made some effort to investigate Iago's allegations, but he is unable to judge what he sees and falls under Iago's greater psychological dominance.

2. Iago has his usual luck in that everyone does the wrong thing at the right moment for Iago.

3. The private tragedy has become public knowledge; evil spreads rapidly; it is infectious.

ACT IV: SCENE 2

In a room within the castle, Othello questions Emilia about Desdemona's activities. She assures him that Desdemona is honest. Cassio has been with her, of course, but never alone. Emilia was never sent to fetch a fan, gloves, mask, or anything else. In short, Emilia insists, she is ready to wager her soul on Desdemona's virtue. "That's strange," Othello reflects, as he sends Emilia to call Desdemona. But as soon as Emilia leaves, Othello decides that, although Emilia has made an adequate defense of her mistress, it is no more than any bawd would do. Besides, Emilia is a subtle whore, who keeps a private room full of villainous secrets on the one hand, and on the other, she will kneel and pray with the most virtuous. Othello says he has seen her do it (that is, pray). And with that, he dismisses her testimony.

Emilia returns, escorting Desdemona. Gently, Othello invites Desdemona to ". . . come hither." Then, dangerously, he tells her to look into his eyes, to show her face. Turning to Emilia, he bids her get to work, close the door, attend to her "mystery" (duty, the function of a madam of a brothel).

Comment

Othello tortures himself in this scene by pretending his wife is a prostitute, Emilia the madam, and he the stranger visiting her.

He urges Desdemona to damn herself by swearing (falsely, he presumes) that she is his wife, and to be "double-damned" by swearing she is honest.

Comment

Here Othello displays his tragic dilemma: Now that suspicion has been engendered, there is no way to get rid of it. If Desdemona says she is faithful, his suspicion will make him doubt her; if she says she is not, she will only confirm his suspicion. He can only believe her if he already trusts her, in which case he would not be suspicious at all.

At last Desdemona realizes that the Moor is jealous. She swears she is faithful but to no avail. Othello is a pathetic sight. He shoos her away and bursts into tears. (Desdemona is thoroughly perplexed; she cannot believe he means his accusations and still thinks "something of moment" is the cause of his suffering. But what connections has that with her?) She asks if he suspects her father, Brabantio, to have been behind his recall to Venice. If so, she implores, he must not blame her, for she too has lost Brabantio's favor. Moved by self-pity, Othello says he could have endured the most painful afflictions, but to be discarded by the woman he has loved or to keep her "as a cistern for foul toads / To knot and gender in" - this is beyond endurance. (The image of adultery as a cistern full of toads is particularly foul and conveys precisely the horror Othello felt for this act. Other horrific images and outrageous epithets follow.) He compares Desdemona's chastity to "summer flies in the shambles"; she is a "fair paper" inscribed with "whore," a "public commoner," an "impudent strumpet," and "heaven stops the nose" at her rank smell. Desdemona asserts her innocence time and again, but she can do nothing with this madman. Sarcastically, Othello apologizes for mistaking her for the "cunning whore of Venice, / That married with Othello," and he calls for Emilia with several equally unsavory epithets. Concluding his fantastic conception (the pretense that he is visiting a brothel), he pays Emilia the madam's fee and asks her to unlock the door and keep secret his visit.

Othello is clearly maddened with grief and has devised a fantastic playlet (like modern psychodrama), in which he acts out his fears that Desdemona is a whore, that Emilia is her bawd, and that men pay to visit his wife. The scene is all the more horrific in that Othello is the only player and ladies are defenseless against his loathsome epithets and lewd insinuations. The maggots of filth have taken over Othello's disintegrating mind.

Othello leaves Desdemona totally dazed; she describes her condition to Emilia as "half-asleep." (She has been through a nightmare and has not yet fully awakened.) In a grotesque bit of word-play on "my lord" and "thy lord," Desdemona pathetically argues with Emilia that since "my lord" is the same man to both of them, Emilia's lord, Iago, is Desdemona's lord too. She orders that her wedding sheets be put upon her bed and that Iago be called.

Desdemona's grim jest is most appropriate at this point. It shows that she has reached the very bottom of despair from which there is nowhere else to go but up. Her feelings are beyond tears. The jest, like Othello's fantasy, hinges on the **theme** of adultery. Her chastity, having been denied so violently, becomes an appropriate subject, Desdemona feels, for her own game of "adulteress." Her request for an interview with Iago

appears aptly in the context of her pathetic jest, but it is also a
real request, for she hopes that Iago can help her.

Emilia returns promptly with Iago. Desdemona is too full of
self-pity at this point to state her wishes clearly. Emilia tells Iago
that Othello has abused and "bewhored" Desdemona. Desdemona
asks, "Am I that name, Iago?" (Delicately, she refuses to use the
word "whore.") Covering his malicious delight, Iago innocently
asks, "What name, fair lady?" But Desdemona is evasive, "Such
as she says my lord did say I was." Emilia, suffering from fewer
inhibitions, bluntly states. "He call'd her whore." A fine thing,
indeed, Emilia broods, to call a woman whore who has refused
fashionable marriages, and has left her father and her country
to be with her husband. With sarcastic virulence, Emilia repeats
all the inquiries Othello had made of her. Finally, Emilia states
her suspicion that some slanderer has been at work. She tells
Iago that it was some such "base notorious knave" that caused
him to suspect her with the Moor.

Comment

Desdemona seems to be too dazed to notice this remark, for if
she had heard it she would have been embarrassed by it at the
least. Emilia, who genuinely loves her mistress, is outraged at
Othello's treatment of her. She does not yet suspect Iago. We
may be learning here that Emilia's and Desdemona's alleged
adulteries were invented by the same villain.

In another piece of dramatic **irony**, Desdemona asks Iago
for advice. How can she win her lord again, she asks the villain.
Iago tells her not to worry; it is some business of state that has
caused him to act this way. Trumpets sound, announcing dinner

which the Venetian envoys are to attend. Desdemona and Emilia leave for it.

The scene concludes with a conversation between Roderigo and Iago. Roderigo has begun to suspect Iago. He tells him that "your words and performances are not kin together"; Iago's words and deeds do not correspond. Roderigo has given Iago enough jewels for Desdemona to corrupt a nun. (Obviously, the jewels have been pocketed by Iago.) Roderigo threatens to demand them of Desdemona. If they are forthcoming, he will repent his "unlawful solicitation" if not, he will demand satisfaction of Iago. Iago devises another impromptu scheme. Othello will be leaving with Desdemona, unless some accident causes him to stay. Now, if Cassio were removed, if he were incapable of taking Othello's place, the Moor and his wife would have to stay on Cyprus. If Roderigo, will undertake to knock out Cassio's brains, Iago will be there to second him. It is high supper time as the scene ends.

SUMMARY

This scene accomplishes the following dramatic purposes:

1. It illustrates the progress of Othello's degradation (the brothel scene) and prepares us for his nadir, when he becomes a murderer.

2. It serves to accentuate the nobility, innocence, and tenderness of Desdemona doth in the terrible confrontation with her husband and in her conversation with Iago.

3. The machinery of the plot is running down. Othello is prepared for murder; Desdemona is prepared to

be cast off; Iago is arranging to have Roderigo and Cassio finish each other off (but the villain will be foiled); Emilia is prepared to expose her mistress' slanderer (and will pay for her loyalty with her life).

4. Preparation is made for Iago's downfall in the next and last act. The height of **irony** is reached when Desdemona appeals to Iago for help. After this, Iago's powers can only decline. Emilia's rage will turn against her husband when she finally uncovers his villainy, and Roderigo's incipient rebellion against Iago augurs the downfall of the villain.

ACT IV: SCENE 3

Othello, Lodovico, Desdemona, Emilia, and attendants are assembled in another room in the castle. As the scene opens the supper has ended and Lodovico is taking his leave. Othello offers to walk with his guest part of his way. He orders Desdemona to go to bed for the night, to dismiss Emilia, and await his return.

Comment

Shakespeare, having reduced the maddened Othello to a most pitiable spectacle, next imparts pathos to Desdemona.

When the ladies are left alone, Emilia remarks that Othello looks gentler than he did before. (This is the calm before the next storm.) Desdemona asks for her nightclothes and hurriedly prepares for bed, for fear of displeasing her husband. As she undresses, she expresses her love for the Moor even though he is stubborn, scolding, and angry. Emilia reports that she has laid the bed with the wedding sheets as Desdemona had ordered. As if presaging doom, Desdemona's thoughts fly to death. She asks Emilia to shroud her in her wedding sheets should she die before her attendant. Then she tells Emilia bout a song she once learned from her mother's maid-a girl called Barbary-whose lover went insane and forsook her. The song is called "Willow." It is an old song, Desdemona recalls, "but it express'd her fortune, / And she died singing it." That song has been in her mind all night. She has all she can do to keep from singing it, Desdemona says, and she tries to forget her troubles with idle chatter about Lodovico. But the diversion doesn't work, and Desdemona sings poignantly: "The poor soul sat sighing by a sycamore tree, / Sing all a green willow."

Comment

Desdemona is in a state of morbid trepidation. She speaks of death, arranges for her shroud, and recalls the story of the young maid Barbary (possibly because she was black) whose situation obviously parallels her own. Desdemona cannot get Barbary's death-song out of her mind. Psychologically, Desdemona is displaying apprehension dramatically; she is **foreshadowing** her death.

Desdemona asks Emilia whether there actually are women who commit adultery; she would not do such a thing for all the world. Emilia replies, "The world's a huge thing. It is a great price for a small vice." She would not do such a thing for a trifle, but "who would not make her husband a cuckold to make him a monarch?" In a more serious vein, Emilia argues that it is the indifference and misbehavior of husbands that lead women to sin. Emilia's thesis is that women have the right to live by the same moral standard as men.

Comment

Emilia, though basically a decent person, is more realistic than Desdemona and has a coarser sense of humor. Her earthy values serve as a contrast to the idealism of Desdemona.

SUMMARY

This scene serves the following dramatic objectives:

1. The scene provides a psychological pause after the tensions built up during the preceding action. Desdemona's poignantly beautiful lyric serves as a lull before the next storm.

2. It emphasizes the noble innocence of Desdemona by contrasting it with the earthy **realism** of Emilia.

3. It makes Desdemona the object of our pity and deepens the tragedy of her impending death.

4. It creates suspense by effecting a delay between Othello's decision to kill Desdemona and the actual killing.

5. It heightens the enormity of Othello's crime by providing time for his premeditation and eliminating the possibility that Othello murders in the heat of passion.

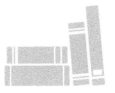

OTHELLO

ACT 5

....

ACT V: SCENE 1

The scene shifts to a street in Cyprus near Bianca's house. Iago and Roderigo are preparing to ambush Cassio. Roderigo has misgivings about murdering Cassio, but he reasons that death is merely the departure of a man, and this murder may bring him satisfying results. Iago is also uncertain about the outcome, but he sees enormous gains no matter what happens. Roderigo is to do the actual killing; if Roderigo survives, Iago will have to restore the jewels intended for Desdemona and which Iago has misappropriated. It is to Iago's advantage that Roderigo dies in the encounter with Cassio. Cassio's death is also desirable, for "he hath a daily beauty in his life / That makes me ugly." Besides, Cassio would expose Iago's lies to Othello if he ever learned of them. No, Iago must have them both out of the way.

Comment

Among his other villanies, Iago emerges here as an uninhibited killer. This is also the first time Iago shows concern for his own safety and expresses fear of exposure. This m y be taken an another forecast of Iago's imminent downfall.

Cassio arrives; Roderigo attacks. As he feared, Roderigo's onslaught is unsuccessful. In fact, Cassio is protected by a coat of mail and succeeds in wounding Roderigo. Iago now emerges from concealment, wounds Cassio in the leg, and flees. Othello, hearing Cassio's cries, is delighted with Iago's work ("O brave Iago, honest and just / That hast such a noble sense of they friend's wrong"). He leaves without examining Cassio's supposed corpse.

Both wounded men lie on different parts of the stage, calling for help. At a distance, Lodovico and Gratiano hear their shouts. Iago returns with a light and finds Cassio. "What villains have done this?" he asks. Iago calls Lodovico and Gratiano to help Cassio and goes off in "search for the bloody thieves." Finding Roderigo, Iago stabs him to death. Lodovico commends Iago on his timely action, and all turn to assist Cassio. Roderigo's last words have been, "O damned Iago! O inhuman dog!"

Comment

Roderigo has been the first to suspect Iago of double-dealing; now he is the first to realize his betrayal and condemn the traitor. Other recognitions will follow.

Bianca rushes out of her lodging and is terribly distraught. On the spur of the moment, Iago decides to implicate Bianca in the ambush of Cassio. He tells the gentlemen that he suspects "this trash / To a part in this injury." Next, he feigns the discovery of Roderigo, whom the Venetians, Lodovico and Gratiano, know. Through artfully phrased question, Iago continues to cast suspicion on Bianca for engineering the death of Roderigo. Cassio is put in a chair, and the General's surgeon is called.

Emilia arrives and learns from Iago that Cassio's misfortunes are "the fruits of whoring." There is a brief exchange between the two women in which Bianca claims (perhaps with justice) to be as honest as Emilia. Bianca freely admits that Cassio "supp'd" at her house, and Iago uses this statement to charge her with the crime. Emilia is sent to inform Othello and Desdemona of the disaster, and Iago (once more **foreshadowing** his own fall) privately expresses doubt: "This is the night / That either makes me or fordoes me quite."

SUMMARY

This brief scene is filled with action; it completes the resolution of the play and prepares us for the conclusion.

1. Iago has succeeded in a minor objective-ridding himself of Roderigo and saving himself the embarrassment of accounting for the jewels.

2. He has not succeeded in a major objective-ridding himself of Cassio. Iago's fortune is beginning to change. Hitherto, accident and coincidence have always worked in his favor. This time, Lodovico's and Gratiano's untimely arrival has prevented Iago from finishing off Cassio.

3. Iago is as quick-witted as ever in turning opportunity to his advantage. Bianca, because of her reputation as a prostitute, easily falls into his net. (Shakespeare has too many things to consider in the crowded canvas of his last act to bother with Bianca again. Presumably, she is exonerated. She is implicated in the crime here in order to stress Iago's restless capacity for intrigue and evil.)

ACT V: SCENE 2

The final scene of the play shifts to a chamber in Othello's castle. Desdemona is in bed. Carrying a candle, Othello enters. He sees Desdemona asleep and beings to speak: "It is the cause, it is the cause, my soul."

Comment

This fatal scene opens with a poignant and magnificent speech by Othello. He has recovered some of his composure, which he had originally possessed when "the full senate found [him] all in all sufficient."

Othello uses the word "cause" (guilt, reason for punishment) in its legal sense. The word suggests that Othello has made a judicial decision, reached after a careful examination and evaluation of the evidence. Othello does not want to commit a "crime of passion" or an act of revenge (a kind of "wild justice" as Francis Bacon defined it.) He has always taken pride in his own restraint, his cool command, and his sense of justice. Now he brings these qualities to bear in his calculated decision to execute Desdemona, "else she'll betray more men."

Othello declares that he will not name the "cause" to the "chaste" stars. Looking down on fair Desdemona, he declines to shed her blood or scar "that whiter skin of hers than snow / And smooth as monumental alabaster." (He plans suffocation, which leaves no marks.)

Comment

A good deal of the play takes place in the night where monstrous thoughts are engendered and brought to light (cf. I.iii.409-10). Images of light are woven into the dark fabric of this final scene to heighten by contrast the blackness of tragic events.

Murder must be done, and darkness is needed for the crime. "Put out the light, and then put out the light," Othello says, addressing the candle. Playing on two meanings of the word "light," (1. candlelight; 2. light of life), Othello says, "If I quench thee / the taper / . . . / I can again thy former light restore." But the light of Desdemona, once extinguished, is out forever. He addresses Desdemona as a "pattern of excelling nature" and compares her to a rose, which, once plucked, must wither. Moved by his reflections, he kisses his sleeping wife. So affecting is that kiss that Othello is tempted to break his sword of "justice." He is even brought to tears, cruel tears, but he soon regains his former resolve.

Desdemona wakens and timidly asks, "Will you come to bed, my lord?" (Stern in his sense of justice, Othello does not want to damn Desdemona's soul.) "Have you pray'd?" he asks. He urges her to confess her sins before being killed. "Talk you of killing"? Desdemona asks, apprised for the first time in the play of Othello's full intentions. "Heaven have mercy on me," Desdemona cries. She expresses her hope that he does not mean this, but she sees the rolling of his eyes and is reduced to terror. At last Othello tells her the cause of his anger: "That handkerchief which I so lov'd and gave thee / Thou gav'st to Cassio." Sensibly, she tells him to send for the man and ask him. She pleads with Othello, telling him that she never did offense to him in her life, never loved Cassio "but with such general warranty of heaven / As I might love." Angrily, Othello responds that he himself saw Cassio with the handkerchief in his hand. His fury increasing, he blames Desdemona for turning his sacrifice into a murder, that is, for making him angry so that he will kill in passion and not in cool justice. (He regards the calculated killing as a "sacrifice" to the God of justice.) As for Cassio, he is dead. Ambiguously, Desdemona cries, "Alas! he is betray'd and I undone." She burst into tears, which Othello interprets as grief for Cassio: "Out, strumpet! Weep'st thou for him to my face?" Smothering her pleas for mercy, he kills her before she has prayed.

Suddenly, there is a knocking at the door. It is Emilia coming to report Roderigo's death and the attack on Cassio. The knocking continues as Othello tries to make sure that Desdemona does not linger in pain. "By-and-by," Othello calls, assuring himself that Desdemona is dead. He surmises correctly that Emilia has come to report on Cassio: "If she come in, she'll sure speak to my wife." Suddenly, the awful realization occurs. "My wife! my wife! I have no wife." (These words recall Desdemona's grim jest on the loss of "my lord" and echo hollowly in the death chamber.)

Emilia continues to call. In a moment, Othello answers, drawing the curtains around Desdemona's corpse. Emilia enters with the news, that foul murder has been done. Before she can finish her message, Othello sums up the deeds of the night:

. . . It is the very error of the moon; She come more nearer earth than she was wont, And makes men mad.

Comment

Emilia's knocking at the door to bring news in the midst of the murder is the same technique Shakespeare used in the knocking at the gate scene in *Macbeth*.

A death cry comes from Desdemona, "O, falsely, falsely murther'd." Emilia discovers her dying mistress; "O who hath done this deed?" she cries. "Nobody, I myself," Desdemona gasps before she dies. Othello feigns innocence momentarily, then passionately charges, "She's, like a liar, gone to burning Hell! / 'Twas I that kill'd her." Then her lie makes her more than the angel and Othello the blacker devil for killing such a one, Emilia retorts. They exchange their judgments of Desdemona's virtues and remain deadlocked on either side of the question until Othello says, "Thy husband knew it all." Emilia is stunned. "My husband?" she repeats over and over again. "I say thy husband. Dost understand the word?" Emilia curses Iago's soul and turns her fury against Othello, whom she now calls Desdemona's "filthy bargain."

Emilia yells for help and, at the same time, spits abuses at the Moor: "O gull! O dolt! / As ignorant as dirt!" Montana, Gratiano, Iago, and others respond to her cry. At once Emilia demands that Iago explain and clear himself. Iago equivocates at first, but he is forced to admit that he accused Desdemona. Emilia discloses the murder to the shocked assembly. Gratiano, Desdemona's uncle, finds some consolation in knowing that Brabantio has died before this calamity. Othello explains the cause of the murder and mentions the handkerchief. Now Emilia understands the whole plot. Stricken with shame and remorse, Emilia insists on speaking. Iago draws his sword, threatening to quiet her forever, but Emilia shows the **episode** of the dropped handkerchief in its true light.

Othello runs at Iago when he hears the truth, but he is restrained by Montano and disarmed. Iago stabs Emilia and flees. Now dying, Emilia asks to be buried by the side of her mistress. Montano takes off after the villain, and Gratiano goes to guard the door, leaving Othello and Emilia alone.

Comment

Othello's terrible certainty of his wife's betrayal is revealed as a fantasy. He must now accept the excruciating knowledge that Desdemona was true.

Othello castigates himself for losing his sword to Montano. He feels there is no point in loving now that Desdemona is dead. Meanwhile, Emilia has become delirious and addresses her dead mistress. Singing snatches of the "Willow" song, Emilia defends her mistress to the "cruel Moor" with her dying breath.

Recalling that he has another sword in his chamber, Othello finds it and calls for Gratiano, whom he addresses as "Uncle." When Gratiano enters, Othello shows him the weapon, boasts of his skill in using it, and in a torrent of self-recrimination, mourns for his dead wife.

Comment

Othello wants the sword to prevent anyone from coming to him. He has no desire to fight.

He delivers a long, heart-rending speech. He knows that he has come to the "very sea-mark of my utmost sail"; it is his "journey's end." "Where should Othello go?" he asks. He looks upon the corpse of Desdemona - "O ill-starred wench! / Pale as they smock!" On judgment day the look that she bears in death will send his soul to hell. His surge of wild rhetoric ends in a moan; "O Desdemona! Desdemona! dead! O! O! O!"

Iago is brought back, a prisoner who has in part confessed to his "villainy." Othello succeeds in wounding him on his next try. Then, Othello asks forgiveness of Cassio, who has been brought in on his chair. He wants to know why "that demi-devil," Iago, has ensnared his body and soul. Intractable to the end, Iago replies, "Demand me nothing; what you know, you know / From this time forth I never will speak word." What is not confirmed about Iago's plot by various witnesses is supplied by letters found on the person of Roderigo. The details of the story are clarified but the tragedy cannot be undone.

Othello is to be relieved of his command; he will be returned to Venice as a prisoner until his case is disposed of. But Othello has other plans. In his final speech, he says Venice is aware of the service he has rendered her. Lodovico and the others are to report to him as he truly is, exaggerating nothing, casting malice on nothing: "then must you speak / Of one that lov'd not wisely but too well." Othello punctuates the end of his speech by stabbing himself to death: "Set you down this; . . . / I took by th' throat the circumcised dog / And smote him - thus."

Before dying, Othello addresses the body of Desdemona: "I kiss'd thee ere I killed thee. No way but this - / Killing myself, to die upon a kiss." He falls upon her bed. In the briefest of eulogies, Cassio says, ". . . He was great of heart." Lodovico expresses the feelings of all when he calls Iago, "O Spartan dog / More fell than anguish, hunger, or the sea!" and consigns the "censure of this hellish villain" to Cassio.

Comment

While Othello's final kiss points to some sort of reconciliation with man and suggests the possibility of his religious redemption, the critic Paul Siegel, author of *Shakespearean Tragedy* and the *Elizabethan Compromise*, takes another approach. "In committing self-murder at the conclusion he [Othello] is continuing to follow Judas' example. His behavior in his last moments, therefore, would have confirmed Elizabethans in the impression that his soul is lost, which they observed from the dramatic **irony** of his offering Desdemona an opportunity, as he supposes, for salvation and then withdrawing it in a rage, not realizing that his own salvation is at issue and forgetting that those who do not forgive will not be forgiven."

SUMMARY

The last scene of the play ties up all the loose threads of plot, **theme**, and characterization.

1. Othello intends the killing of Desdemona to be a calculated "sacrifice" to justice, not a murder and a butchery, but he fails in his intention and is forced to kill Desdemona in the heat of anger. Shakespeare shows that Othello does not really regain the self-control which distinguishes him in the early acts of the play.

2. When it is too late, Othello learns the truth from Emilia, that his suspicions are unfounded. During his last moments of life, he knows the anguishing truth. Othello dies, a self-murderer, declaring that he was "one not easily jealous," but "perplex'd in the extreme."

125

> 3. Iago is unmasked by his own wife whom he kills. He refuses to speak further. His powers of destruction finally turn against his own person, and he is destined for torture and execution.

A fitting conclusion to this summary of the tragedy of *Othello* is Dr. Samuel Johnson's evaluation of the play as a whole. No one can say more in a few words: "The beauties of this play impress themselves so strongly upon the attention of the reader, that they can draw no aid from critical illustration. The fiery openness of Othello, magnanimous, artless, ardent in his affection, inflexible in his resolution, and obdurate in his revenge; the cool malignity of Iago, silent in his resentment, subtle in his designs, and studious at once of his interest and his vengeance; the soft simplicity of Desdemona, confident of merit, and conscious of innocence, her artless perseverance in her suit, and her slowness to suspect that she can be suspected, are such proofs of Shakespeare's skill in human nature, as, I suppose, it is vain to seek in any modern writer. The gradual progress which Iago makes in the Moor's conviction, and the circumstances which he employs to inflame him, are so artfully natural, that, though it will not be said of him as he says of himself, that he is a man not easily jealous, yet we cannot but pity him when at last we find him perplexed in the extreme."

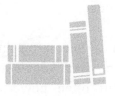

OTHELLO

. . . .

OTHELLO

Shakespeare, in his major work, has a special gift of creating characters about whom no last, definite, and final word can be expressed. There always exists some area of "ambiguity" - the possibility of two meanings, even of multiple meanings. The sensitive reader is left to "ponder"; he experiences the same reaction to a Shakespearean character as he does to people in real life; certain things he definitely knows about them other aspects of the person are left mysterious, shadowed, about which he can only surmise. Characters in a Shakespeare play, like real people, may not completely know themselves; they may have subconscious urges, unexamined attitudes, improvised reactions to new situations. Shakespeare is able to catch this aspect of real experience. His characters have a great degree of "fluidity"; and this is true just as much of a comparatively straightforward character such as Othello as that of a complex, introverted character such as Hamlet.

First, then, let us consider what we obviously know about Othello.

(1) He has been a successful professional soldier, a condottiere of the type well known to Italian Renaissance history. The small, but often powerful, Italian city states frequently engaged free-lance generals, with their own private armies, to do their fighting for them on a contractual basis. Their own citizens preferred to pursue trade and the arts. Venice, in the historical period of *Othello*, was one of the richest states in Europe, its power out of all measure to its geographical size. It had gained its preeminence by roughly corresponding to a great "free port" for the Mediterranean. Traders had confidence that their contracts would be legally enforceable there; that Venetian law, in these respects, was tolerant and international in viewpoint. Shylock, the Merchant of Venice; suffered in certain respects, but there was no impediment to pursuing his business and having recourse to law for the enforcing of his contracts. Nor does the Venetian republic hesitate to place Othello, whom we assure to be a black man, though some maintain he is an Arab in (any event, a man of quite different racial background from that of the Venetians), in supreme command of its armies. What is a little unusual about Othello's appointment is that he is placed in command of Venetians, with Cassio, a Venetian general, second-in-command. There is no mention anywhere in the play of contracted mercenaries. Othello tells us himself that his entire experience has been military. He has lived in camps, engaging in the arts of war, since he was a boy of seven. The only part of the great world that he knows is that which pertains to broils and battles. He has traveled extensively in distant and mysterious regions, including those of the "Cannibals" and the "Anthropophago." He had once been taken prisoner and sold into slavery, but had managed to escape. He has loved the "pride, pomp, and circumstance of glorious war!" He loves its color and glitter - the plumed troops, the neighing steed, the spirit-stirring drum.

talk about his background

Othello takes his part in a definite historical setting. *The Aldus Shakespeare* states: "The island of Cyprus became subject to the republic of Venice in 1471. After this time, the only attempt ever made upon the island by the Turks was under Selim the Second, in 1570. It was then invaded by a powerful force, and conquered in 1571. We learn from the play that there was a junction of the Turkish fleet at Rhodes for the invasion of Cyprus; that is first sailed towards Cyprus, then went to Rhodes, there met another squadron, and then resumed its course to Cyprus. These are historical facts, and took place when Mustapha, Selim's general, attacked Cyprus, in May, 1570; which is therefore the true period of the action." *which destroys later*

(2) The second important fact we know about Othello is that he possesses a "public image" of great dignity (regardless of whether, as some critics maintain, he is inwardly insecure). The Venetian senate unanimously approved of him ("all in all sufficient"). Even Brabantio, who is later to have a bitter quarrel with him, invited him often to his own home. When Brabantio cannot effectively prevent Othello's marriage, he still shows respect and appreciation for Othello ("I here do give thee that with all my heart . . ."). Far from bragging and telling "fantastical lies," as Iago alleges to Rederigo, Othello tells the simple truth without being apologetic or conceited. When Brabantio begins to proceed against him, Othello is unimpressed. He knows that his own services to the "signiory" will "out-tongue his complaints." He is a man of royal ancestry as well as a man who has proved himself by his own achievements. He married Desdemona because he loved her, and refuses to be evasive in regard to Brabantio. "My parts, my title, and my perfect soul / Shall manifest me rightly." When his followers and those of Brabantio are about to get into a bloody conflict, Othello, with a word of command that is also courteous, quiets both sides:

"Good signior, you shall more command with years / Than with your weapons." Before the senate, he recounts the details of his life factually, yet eloquently. His arguments are indisputable, and no one holds what he has done against him. Even the Duke who is presiding, says, "I think this tale would win my daughter, too." He is placed in charge of the war against the Turks. In no way excited or embarrassed by what has occurred, Othello, firmly though ceremoniously, demands that the State arrange suitable accommodation for his wife and proper servants. Obviously, Othello is a person conscious of his own worth. He does not have to be aggressive, "push himself" because of any inferiority complex. He has the maturity required to recognize the legitimate rights and feelings of others. Under normal circumstances, he never degrades anyone. Though he may be a man with a "round, unvarnish'd tale," he has the qualities of a good diplomat, in the higher and more sincere sense of that word.

(3) Another obvious fact about Othello is that he is a "Moor." The full title of the play reads: *The Tragedy of Othello, The Moor of Venice.* The term "Moor" has been in dispute. Coleridge asks, can we imagine Shakespeare "so utterly ignorant as to make a barbarous black man plead royal birth? a Schlegel, on the other hand, pursuing the "noble savage" interpretation of Othello, observes "what a fortunate mistake that the Moor, under which name a baptized Saracen of the northern coast of Africa was unquestionably meant in the novel, has been made by Shakespeare, in every respect, a black man!" A. C. Bradley argues with reference to Coleridge, who had maintained that it would show a lack of balance on the part of Desdemona to fall in love with a black man, that this was just what Brabantio was alleging! Bradley will not go so far as to say that Shakespeare imagined him as a black man and not as a Moor, "for that might imply that he distinguished black mans and Moors precisely as

we do but what appears to me nearly certain is that he imagined Othello as a black man, and not as light-brown one." Marvin Rosenberg observes in The Masks of Othello: "Probably Burbage played Othello black, rather than tawny, for this was the theater tradition that survived unbroken-as Shakespearean traditions usually did, unless an important social or theatrical development intervened-until widespread slavery. Othello changed to "tawny" in the 1800s to free the role from the unfortunate **connotations** borne by that growing social evil, and to preserve the vision of a gallant, high-hearted man whose lineage, though strange, is in no way inferior to that of his hosts, nor is thought so by them. His apartness is a badge, not a shame." Othello's color was meant to have romantic associations. Shakespeare was still close to the medieval tradition where in most delineations of "The Adoration of the Magi" a black man is presented as one of the Kings. He is quite removed from the impact of Puritan Christianity which tended to put certain nationalities and races "outside the pale."

(4) Another obvious fact about Othello is that he is, and was meant to be, a romantic figure. Iago may regard him as a "wheeling and extravagant stranger of here and everywhere," but his adventurous and traveled background stirred the Venetian senate. He brings suggestions of a mysterious non European world, of the Egyptian sibyl who had given his mother the strange handkerchief: "there's magic in the web of it." Two hundred years of the Sibyl's life went into the making of it, "dyed in mummy which the skillful / Conserv'd of maiden's hearts." Othello's public image of discipline an self-control has, in contrast to his adventurous and mysterious background, a special romantic appeal of its own; it is something quite outside ordinary experience. Iago himself is shocked by Othello's anger, because it is so unexpected. "Can he be angry?" he asks. He has seen the cannon "puff" Othello's brother from his very arm, and

he has remained absolutely cool. Adventure, excitement, racial uniqueness, cool head, and cool decision combine to make this romantic image.

(5) It is also clear that Othello's romantic background and his difference in race create certain disadvantages which become important in the action of the play. Shakespeare is not writing a "problem" play about the marriage of a black man and a "white" woman. In fact, the play is so universally human that for long intervals we completely forget about the difference in race. But Iago scores a decisive point by insinuating that Othello really knows very little about Venice and Venetian women. Othello overtly refers to the fact that he is not a "chamberer" intimate with the niceties and intrigues of social life: "for I am black / And have not those soft parts of conversation / That chamberers have . . ."

We now come to examine those major points, relative to the character of Othello, about which knowledge must be "ambiguous" and "fluid."

(1) What is the nature of Othello's love for Desdemona? Robert B. Heilman in Magic in the Webs Action and Language in Othello sees in the play a contest between Othello's vow of love and Iago's "wits" (intellect). "Thou know'st," Iago says, "we work by wit, and not by witchcraft. . . ." Dr. Heilman comments: "Wit and witchcraft: in this antithesis is the symbolic structure, or the thematic form, of Othello. By witchcraft, of course, Iago means conjuring and spells to induce desired actions and states of being. But as a whole the play dramatically develops another meaning of witchcraft and forces upon us an awareness of that meaning: witchcraft is a **metaphor** for love. The 'magic in the web' of the handkerchief, as Othello calls it, extends into the fiber

of the whole drama. Love is a magic bringer of harmony between those who are widely different (Othello and Desdemona), and it can be a magic transformer of personality; its ultimate power is fittingly marked by the miracles of Desdemona's voice speaking from beyond life, pronouncing forgiveness to the Othello who has murdered her. Such events lie outside the realm of 'wit'-of the reason, cunning, and wisdom on which Iago rests - and this wit must be hostile to them." Thus is an articulately sensitive expression of a point of view common in modern criticism: that Othello falls from a great intuitive faith into a complicated rationalizing in which he becomes the easy victim of Iago's "wits."

Why should such a fall take place, unless there was some pre-existing weakness in the quality of his love? Such critics as G. R. Elliott and F. R. Leavis have emphasized a strain of egoism in *Othello* (which may constitute his "tragic flaw," as we shall discuss later). He certainly fails to trust his own intuition in an acute moment of crisis, though it was the same intuition that had led to his unconventional and romantic marriage, "to be free and bounteous to her mind." When Iago has started to poison his mind, Othello catches a glimpse of Desdemona, and exclaims, "if she be false, O, then heaven mocks itself! / I'll not believe 't." That was the right intuition which Othello failed to maintain because, these critics argue, his love was far from being perfected. Of course, viewing the other side of the picture, we have to admit that Othello pays a disproportionate, even a monstrous, price for his lack of perfection. After all, in normal life, a man, as husband and father, grows and deepens in the knowledge of love. If absolute selflessness were a prerequisite to marriage, would anyone qualify? The play indicates pretty clearly that Othello's marriage would have been happy and successful if Othello had not fallen into the hands of so skilled a manipulator as Iago.

(2) We now come specifically to the question of the "tragic flaw" in *Othello*. According to the tradition of tragedy as stated by Aristotle in his *Poetics* (a tradition followed by the Renaissance), the tragic hero must not be an entirely good man, or one who is completely evil, but, rather, a man who on the whole is good but contributes to his own destruction by some moral weakness (the "fatal flaw"). The reason for this, as Aristotle sees it, lies in the emotions that tragedy is meant to excite in the audience. They are "pity" and "fear." If an entirely good man is destroyed, we do not feel pity but indignation with the universe. If an evil man comes to an evil end, we have no feelings in the matter whatever. We think that he got his "just deserts." But we pity the man who, having contributed in some way to his disaster, meets with a punishment out of all proportion to what he has done. "Fear" arises from our anxiety for the character as the play unfolds. We hope against hope that he will succeed in getting out of his difficulty. And, after the disaster is final, we fear for ourselves. For if an Othello, with all his great qualities and achievements, receives such a blow, what might the rest of us expect from life? One critic, Hazelton Spencer, actually cannot locate a tragic flaw in Othello. "Critics have searched for a tragic flaw in Othello, something to justify his miserable end, on the theory that to present the fall of an innocent man is, as Aristotle holds, incapable of arousing and purifying the emotions of pity and fear. Pity is uppermost in this tragedy, all the more because, humanly speaking, Othello is blameless. He is set before us, in his first appearances, as noble and calm. In his dying speech he describes himself as 'one not easily jealous,' and that is clearly the expression that Shakespeare wishes to leave. Othello is a normal man, and the play is not a study of the passion of jealousy. Why, then, does the magnanimous hero fail so wretchedly?" This critic takes the view that it is Othello's business in this play to be deceived, and leaves it more or less at that. Consequently, he finds the play more pathetic than tragic. Rosenberg in *The*

Masks of Othello extends the concept of tragic flaw much more widely than does Aristotle. In effect, he says, to be human is to have a tragic flaw. True, Othello is one of the finest, one of the noblest of men. "But to be the best of men is still to be frail, to be subject to vanity, pride, insecurity, credulity, and the other marks of mortality. So Othello is no sugar hero of romance. He errs terribly. But the artistic design does not require from him an early "sin to bring on retribution; his tragic flaw is that he is human."

IAGO

Everyone is agreed that Iago is an outstanding study in whatever the word "evil" connotes. Some would argue that it is a more effective study than that of Satan in Milton's *Paradise Lost.* Both Iago and Satan are skilled deceivers, accomplished liars, experts in applied psychology, in the manipulation of the innocent. While theologically it might be maintained that Satan creates more havoc, waste, and suffering than Iago, it is long range rather than immediate, generalized rather than specifically personal. Shakespeare's situation creates much more horror. Milton also could have created much more horror, if he had violated Scripture, and showed Adam killing Eve in jealous rage! Behind Satan's action is a clear motive, however unwarranted. To cause Adam to sin is part of a master plan of the war on heaven, the course of which the devils had debated in detail. Behind Iago's actions are only the workings of his own dark mind. Several schools of thought have developed to account for them. One finds Iago humanly explicable-at least in part. This school accepts at least several claims that Iago makes at their face value. For example, Iago had a just grievance in being passed over for promotion in favor of Cassio, that Othello had had actual relations with Iago's wife, and so on. Another school more plausibly brings the apparatus of modern psychiatry and psychoanalysis to bear on the probings of Iago's mind. Some, like A. C. Bradley, find Iago's behavior explicable enough without taking Iago at face value or bringing modern psychological studies to bear. Some follow the "motiveless malignity" tradition of Coleridge. Others resort to identifying Iago with "Satanism" or just regarding him as a dramatic prop, an impetus to action. In the case of Iago, the list of what we know without question about him is comparatively brief. Besides these things, and the over-all conviction that he is evil as anyone can be, nearly everything else that is said about him must fall within the label of "ambiguous."

As in the case of Othello, we shall start with the facts we know. First, we must realize that it is difficult to distinguish fact from fiction in what Iago says. As A. C. Bradley puts it, "One must constantly remember not to believe a syllable that Iago utters on any subject, including himself, until one has tested his statement by comparing it with known facts and with other statements of his own or other people, and by considering whether he had in the particular circumstances any reason for telling a lie or telling the truth." We know that Iago is "his Moorship's Ancient." We can rely on his statement that he applied for the higher position of lieutenant-General, but not for his account of the qualifications of Cassio, or the reasons for the rejections of Iago's application. We can reasonably infer, from Shakespeare's sources (though not from any explicit statement in the play), that he is handsome, superficially attractive ("a man of the most handsome person . . . very dear to the Moor . . . . he cloaked with proud and valorous speech . . . the villainy of his soul with such art that he was to all outward show another Hector or Achilles"), a man of about twenty-eight years of age. In the play itself, he expresses, in exchange with others, sharp and bantering wit. He has successfully and deliberately created an image of his own straightforwardness and trustworthiness. "Honest" is practically his first name. He is married to Emilia, who is the "lady-in-waiting" to Desdemona.

A. C. Bradley suspects that Iago did not have an aristocratic background, and that his wife is "almost in the relation of a servant to Desdemona." The play really makes nothing clear on this point. Desdemona is sufficiently important socially to have an "aristocratic" lady-in-waiting in her train, which we can reasonably suppose is limited in number because of the military conditions under which Desdemona was permitted to go to the front in Cyprus with Othello. In any event, Iago's public image is geared to that of the "soldier" rather than to that of the "gentleman." We can take as his true views Iago's contemptuous comments on others-Roderigo is a "snipe" only to be used for "sport and profit"; the Moor is to be led by the nose like a jackass; and so on. More difficult to assess are Iago's expressions of genuine admiration ("The Moor . . . is of a constant, loving, noble nature"; Desdemona is "fram'd as fruitful / As the free elements"). We can subscribe to the theory that Iago actually recognizes goodness, truth, beauty in an objective way, and the consciously rejects them:

So will I turn her virtue into pitch, And out of her own goodness make the net That shall enmesh them all.

But it is also possible that Iago performs "chorus" functions. Some of his comments are detached and universal, not necessarily in his proper dramatic person as Iago. Neither, of course, of these interpretations is necessarily inconsistent with the other. We also know that Iago is a killer, that he hates Othello, but his motivations are "ambiguous." We have now come to the end of the list of what we know for certain.

We come to consider the wide area of ambiguity of more uncertainty connected with Iago.

(1) One school of critics is prepared to accept Iago's allegation that Othello has committed adultery with Iago's wife, Emilia. Actually, Iago says "I know not if't be true; / But I, for mere suspicion in that kind, / Will do as for a surety." Later in the play he voices a similar suspicion about Cassio: "For I fear Cassio with my night-cap too . . ." Yet at no point in the play does Iago express any indignation about his wife. He kills her in the last act, but for quite different reasons-she is confirming the evidence against him. Might not Shakespeare's point be that malice comes first, a shaky rationalization afterwards? Once Iago hates Othello, is he prepared to believe any hatred-bearing fantasy against him? To the acceptance of Othello's adultery is sometimes added the assumption that Cassio was preferred over Iago for the appointment to the lieutenancy because Cassio had been the "go-between" in Othello's wooing of Desdemona (there is certainly no statement to this effect in the play). As one critic puts it, "once outer motivations for Iago are accepted, he can be seen as a relatively decent man plunging for the first time into wickedness. . . ." But bo"h the text and the test of the theater itself are against this point of view.

(2) Interpretations of Iago in the light of modern psychological analysis are more fruitful. He is "sick," "disturbed," a "vindictive neurotic." Believing in the supremacy of the will and of the intelligence, with scarcely any ability really to "relate" to people, he sees them merely as objects he must compulsively exploit. He is not neurotic in the way it might be argued that Milton's Satan is. He is not seeking for public and cosmic glory. But like Satan, he is seeking absolute mastery. The words of Clara Thompson in *An Outline of Psychoanalysis* apply well to Iago: "The neurotic loses in the process [i.e. that of seeking absolute mastery] his interest

in truth, a loss that among others accounts for his difficulty in distinguishing between genuine feelings, beliefs, striving, and their artificial equivalents (unconscious pretenses). The emphasis shifts from being to appearing." The neurotic "must develop a system of private values which determines what to like and accept in himself, what to be proud of. But this system of values must by necessity also determine what to reject, to abhor, to be ashamed of, to despise, to hate. Pride and self-hate belong inseparably together; they are two expressions of the same process." Rosenberg in *The Masks of Othello* quotes Karen Horney's *Neurosis and Human Growth* much to the same effect: "Love, compassion, considerateness-all human ties-are felt as restraints on the path to sinister glory . . . he must prove his own worth to himself." Such analysis supports, rather than opposes, William Hazlitt's remark that "Iago is an amateur of tragedy in real life" and the argument of A. C. Bradley that Iago's sense of superiority wanted satisfaction.

(3) A. C. Bradley has undertaken in *Shakespearean Tragedy* to show that Iago's character is quite explicable. While Bradley does not go in for psychological terminology, his analysis is in itself basically psychological though always in reference to actual events in the text. Bradley emphasizes Iago's enormous self-control allied to his belief that absolute egoism is the only rational and proper attitude, and that conscience or honor of any kind of regard for others is an absurdity. Bradley does not consider Iago ambitious; he is not envious in the sense that competitors outrun him. He is only highly competitive (and dangerous without scruples) when his sense of superiority is wounded. He does not care for Emilia, but, on the other hand, he becomes furious at the thought of another man "getting the better of him." Bradley argues that Iago does not love evil for evil's sake, but he does regard goodness as stupid. Goodness weakens his satisfaction with himself, "and disturb his faith that egoism

BRIGHT NOTES STUDY GUIDE

is the right and proper thing." Bradley cannot find any passion in Iago, neither of ambition nor of hatred. As good a summary as any of Bradley's detailed position lies in these words: "Iago stands supreme among Shakespeare's evil characters because the greatest intensity and subtlety of imagination have gone to his making, and because he illustrates in the most perfect combination the two facts concerning evil which seem to have impressed Shakespeare most. The first of these is the fact that perfectly sane people exist in whom fellow-feeling of any kind is so weak that an almost absolute egoism becomes possible to them, and with it those hard vices-such as ingratitude and cruelty-which to Shakespeare were far the worst. The second is that such evil is compatible, and even appears to ally itself easily, with exceptional powers of will and intellect."

A more recent critic, Marvin Rosenberg, who believes that Iago is perfectly understandable in terms of neurosis, elaborates an insight in quite an opposite direction to that of Bradley. He makes an important distinction between the Iago in dialogue with other people and the Iago of the soliloquies. The latter, he says, reveals a "raging torment." "Far from being passionless, this inner Iago is one of great fury of passion, the more furious because so much feeling has been smothered when he is with people."

(4) Coleridge actually leans to the "Satanism" view of Iago, for, in his opinion, Iago is "next to devil, and only not quite devil." But he is one of the first major critics to suggest that it is rather pointless to seek human reasons for Iago's behavior. Elmer Edgar Stoll thinks that we should regard Iago as a necessary "impetus" to the dramatic action, and not try to prod him rationalistically. He is the villain by dramatic necessity, and would have been so accepted by the Elizabethan playgoer. Hazelton Spencer has argued that Iago has to be accepted in terms of centuries of

English stage-villainy. He belongs to the tradition of the devil of medieval history plays, of Judas, of the bad angels, of the Vice of the morality plays. These did not receive or require "any accounting for." The trouble about this point of view is that most readers of Shakespeare find Iago far too absorbing to leave him on this level. He seems to cry out for explanations!

(5) We come, lastly, to various religious or quasi-religious interpretations of Iago. Most religiously-minded people have been brought up in a Socratic interpretation of evil. If a man has the proper knowledge, he will seek the good. No man can deliberately seek evil, though he may actually pursue evil under the mistaken impression that it is the good. Though man by his nature seeks the good, he may be misled into seeking a "mistaken" good. "Evil, be thou my good" is considered a Satanic principle rather than a human possibility. Of course, the possibility has to be recognized (certainly in medieval and Renaissance literature) that sin and intellectual degeneration to some extent correlate. This is the situation present in Christopher Marlowe's Dr. Faustus and in Milton's Satan. The more they fall into evil, the less capable are they of making realistic judgments, though, ironically, they become more cocksure of themselves. A man may not start out by choosing evil for its own sake, but, by degrees and increasing involvement in sin, his judgment becomes impaired so that he fails to distinguish between good and evil. Goodness may challenge, disturb, embarrass, and be overtly rejected. Iago goes pretty far along the Satanic route when he thinks of using Desdemona's goodness as the "net that shall enmesh them all." This would seem to be a statement that could not be relegated to his "chorus" function. Of course, we get into a difficult problem of words if we maintain that a man who hates goodness is really insane. It is hard to set up a firm definition of insanity; such definitions depend upon social **convention** to a great degree. On the surface, Iago seems sane

enough. But one aspect of mental illness permits unimpeded use of the intellect while a man's emotional life is in ruins. This is pretty much Iago's position.

An important school of Shakespearean critics finds religious symbolism in all Shakespeare's great works. Paul Siegel in *Shakespearean Tragedy* and the *Elizabethan Compromise* has interpreted *Othello* against a background of Christian theology. Iago has something of the function of Judas. Robert Heilman also sees Iago functioning as the enemy of salvation. "His most far-reaching method is to seduce others philosophically - to woo them from assumptions in which their salvation might lie (faith in the spiritual quality of others), to baser assumptions that will destroy them (their freedom to act in the light of the accepted unregeneracy of all about them). Iago the moral agent is akin to Iago the philosopher there is a common element in stealing purses, stealing good names, and stealing ideas needed for survival."

DESDEMONA

Though Desdemona is by no means a "simple" character, she is the least involved in ambiguity of any in the play. We know, from Othello's words, that she is the "gentle" Desdemona. As the daughter of a distinguished member of the Venetian oligarchy, she had her choice of suitors among the "wealthy, curled darlings of our nation." Emilia, in that terrible scene in which Othello shouts "whore" at Desdemona, reminds us that she has "forsook so many noble matches, / Her father and her country and her friends." Brabantio describes his daughter as "a maiden never bold; / Of spirit so still and quiet, that her motion / Blushed at herself." He just cannot understand how such an apparently quiet and dutiful girl could do anything so audacious as to elope with Othello. How could she err "against all rules of nature"?

In the investigation of Brabantio's charges against Othello before the Senate, Desdemona speaks softly but with determined authority:

. . . My noble father, I do perceive here a divided duty: To you I am bound for life and education. My life and education both do learn me How to respect you; you are the lord of duty; I am hitherto your daughter: but here's my husband, And so much duty as my mother show'd To you, preferring you before her father, So much I challenge that I may profess Due to the Moor my lord.

This is a lucid explanation of the duties of children to parents and of married people to one another-firm, and only offensive in the degree that real facts are offensive. Brabantio has nothing further to say on the subject: "on to state affairs." If there be some suspicion as the play develops that Desdemona lacked judgment and enterprise in her handling of Othello, she certainly exhibits perfect poise and confidence in the beginning. She acts with tact and originality in asking the Duke to assist her in making a request, while at the same she makes clear, without apology, the nature of her love for Othello. "That I did love the Moor to live with him / My downright violence and storm of fortunes / May trumpet to the world." She wants permission to go with Othello to Cyprus, otherwise "the rites for which I love him are bereft me." She is frank, unaffected, economical, and to the point. Brabantio's remarks towards the end of the scene are not strictly in keeping with his previous generosity in acceding to a state of facts about the elopement ("I here do give thee that with all my heart"):

Look to her, Moor, if thou hast eyes to see: She has deceiv'd her father, and may thee.

This is a dramatic **foreshadowing** or premonition (illusory in fact) that in no way compromises Desdemona's absolute honesty. Iago is later to makes use of the allegation that Desdemona deceived her father.

When we next see her, she has arrived in Cyprus before Othello. Having been welcomed by Cassio and Montano, she engages in some relaxing banter with Iago. This is carried on with perfect propriety, but it shows that Desdemona is not timid and retiring, a shy violet. She greets the disembarked Othello with a mature sense of what marriage and being a wife mean. "The heavens forbid / But that our loves and comforts should increase, / Even as our days do grow!"

When we see Desdemona on stage again, she has been listening to Cassio's plea for reinstatement into Othello's good graces. Our first impression that Desdemona is a determined girl, having known her own mind in her elopement with Othello, is here confirmed again:

I give thee warrants of thy place: assure thee, If I do vow a friendship, I'll perform it To the last article . . .

Desdemona appears briefly during the course of the temptation scene (III, iii) just long enough for the handkerchief to be dropped - the **episode** that becomes so important a part of the machinery of the plot. When Othello sees her again, she has no reason to suspect the chain of events that have been set in motion against her, With typical single-mindedness she pursues the subject of Cassio's reinstatement while Othello, now poisoned by Iago, is concerned with one thing only, the whereabouts of the handkerchief. She lies in saying that the handkerchief is not lost, paying little heed to its importance. She is amazed when Othello storms off in anger. In a rather typical way of wives dealing with the tantrums of husbands, she assumes that business of some kind must have upset him.

The fact has to be realized that Desdemona is trapped in a very fast movement of events. Iago's plot has worked with lightning speed in less than one "dramatic" day. Desdemona has had only brief and casual moments with her husband; she has had no reason to anticipate such an outburst as that of Othello storming into her apartment and calling her "a public commoner" (IV, ii). She already knows that something is seriously wrong, for Othello had already publicly struck her, but she continues to think of the cause as some temporary nervous derangement based upon frustration in the running of his affairs. "If haply you my father do suspect / An instrument of this your calling back, / Lay not your blame on me: if you have lost him, / Why, I have lost him too." In answer to Othello's angry charge, what else can she do but to express a firm, straightforward denial?

If to preserve this vessel for my lord From any other foul unlawful touch Be not to be a strumpet, I am none.

A modern reader would be unhistorical if he expected a Desdemona to say something like "what in the deuce is the matter with you, Othello? You had better see your psychiatrist at once." An almost ritualistic courtesy is part of the Shakespearean world. This creates a sense of dignity, but also too much distance at times for the kind of "in-fighting" that human life requires. Desdemona always refers to Othello as her "lord": "I hope my noble lord esteems me honest." Her immediate reaction to Othello's behavior is one of numb shock.

In a following sequence, she ironically confides in Iago, asking him, "What shall I do to win my lord again?" Shakespeare emphasizes two facts about Desdemona in this exchange. With all her straightforwardness and courage, Desdemona is extremely sensitive; she cannot use the word "whore." But with that keen moral sensitivity is combined a love of that deep kind which Shakespeare has described elsewhere in one of his sonnets:

. . . Love is not love Which alters when it alteration finds Or bends with the remover to remove (**Sonnet** CXVI)

Even if Othello shakes her off to "beggarly divorcement," even if "unkindness may do much," nothing will "taint" her love.

Desdemona orders her wedding sheets to be placed upon her bed. Shakespeare emphasizes this gesture as a symbol of peace and reconciliation, though ironically Desdemona is to lie murdered upon them. Singing the "willow" song, still unaware of any more immediate menace than the wind knocking upon the door, she thinks, in a rather detached way, of the meaning of adultery. She would not do such a wrong "for the whole world." Shakespeare contrasts Desdemona's exalted standards with those of the practical and down-to-earth Emilia: "Why, the wrong is but a wrong i' the world; and having the world for your labor, 'tis a wrong in your own world, and you might quickly make it right."

Some critics have felt that Desdemona says the "wrong things" on her deathbed. Actually, Desdemona seems very much in character." Shakespeare skillfully indicates how entirely subjective, how entirely belonging to the world of Iago-induced fantasy, is Othello's reaction to her words. Realistically, and with complete poise, she tells Othello to send for Cassio and to ask whether she ever gave him the handkerchief. She does not know that Othello believes him to be dead. Her statement, "Alas! he is betray'd and I undone," indicates a perfectly natural and sudden realization of a plot against her. She bursts into tears - the first time this is indicated in the play. After the mounting tension, this would be in keeping with a personality as determined and as poised as hers. Shakespeare underlines Othello's complete subjectivity by causing him to refer the terms immediately to the presumed death of Cassio: "Out, strumpet! weep'st thou for him to my face?" Othello, beside himself, smothers her without allowing her time for prayer. Emilia knocks at the door; Othello finds Desdemona not quite dead; he returns to his work. In the presence of Emilia, Desdemona has breath enough to say, "a guiltless death I die."

A. C. Bradley states that the suffering of Desdemona is, "unless I mistake, the most intolerable spectacle that Shakespeare offers us. For one thing, it is mere suffering; and . . . that is much worse to witness than suffering that issues in action. Desdemona is helplessly passive. . . . She is helpless because her nature is infinitely sweet and her love absolute." We feel that Bradley exaggerates Desdemona's passiveness. The speed with which development takes place, and with which Desdemona is not directly connected, is an important element to consider. A. C. Bradley himself points out that Othello murdered his wife within a few days, probably a day and a half, of his arrival in Cyprus and the consummation of his marriage. Shakespeare is not technically accurate about time, and actually the audience has an impression of longer time lapses. But the point is that events are meant to move with an almost incredible swiftness. Insofar as Desdemona is passive, she had little time to orientate herself to what everything was about. But her character, as the facts indicated above show, was not normally passive.

Marvin Rosenberg does not believe in pressing the image of a "heavenly" Desdemona in contrast to Iago's "diabolism." He puts what seems to be the facts rather eloquently: "It seems to me as dangerous to rob Desdemona of her human frailty as it is to steal her essential goodness from her. Fortunately for the long life of Shakespeare's play, she no more personifies divinity than deceit. . . . But we care intensely for this young, passionate woman who ran away secretly from her father's house to the arms of her lover, who has a healthy desire to be with her husband on her wedding night, who cries when she is struck, and who fears death terribly. Divinity is beyond our pity; but we weep for the mortal woman who was Desdemona."

EMILIA

A. C. Bradley, in his analysis of Emilia, has one observation of particular relevance: "She is the only person who utters for us the violent common emotions which we feel . . ." "Terror and pity are here too much to bear; we long to be allowed to utter indignation, if not rage; and Emilia lets us feel them and give them words." Emilia is an "army" wife, used to the hard and concrete facts of her husband's profession, without possessing much in the way of imagination, but having firm convictions and common sense. She cares little for social veneers, and speaks her mind without hesitation if the situation demands it. She is the "honest" wife who is the counterpart to the "honest" Iago (except, of course, that she is genuinely "honest") - rough-hewn, frank. Iago had had evidently similar suspicions about her marital loyalty as Othello had in regard to Desdemona, but she must have had the skill to handle this tough specimen of humanity. In Act IV, ii, she turns to her husband, after voicing her conviction that "some base notorious knave" had incited Othello against his wife, declaring:

...Some such squire he was That turn'd your wit the seamy side without, And made you to suspect me with the Moor.

She does not become important in the play until the fourth and fifth acts. She has, however, been instrumental in finding the handkerchief and passing it on to Othello (III, iii). She neglected to reveal that she knew its whereabouts when Othello demanded it (III, iv). From her own experience in marriage she seems to have acquired a generally hostile attitude towards men: 'Tis not a year or two shows us a man: They are all but stomachs, and we all but food; They eat us hungerly, and when they are full, They belch us.

She becomes intensely indignant at Othello's treatment of Desdemona (IV, ii). In the "willow" scene (IV, iii) she does her best to comfort and console Desdemona. She also protests against the "double" sexual standard of men. Women also have "affections, / Desires for sport, and frailty." If men do not observe standards, women are not likely to, either.

Emilia is the first to arrive at the bedchamber of the murdered Desdemona, where Othello is still standing. Othello proclaims his deed, even when the dying Desdemona has exculpated him by saying that she did it herself. In fact he refers to her statement as further proof of what a liar she is! Othello refers to her husband, Iago, as the source of his knowledge. Emilia, in an utter trauma, keeps repeating "my husband!" Emilia, unlike Othello, has no doubts about her own powers of intuition:

If he say so, may his pernicious soul Rot half a grain a day! he lies to the heart: She was too fond of her most filthy bargain.

She remorselessly lashes into Othello: "O gull! O dolt! / As ignorant as dirt!" Emilia "smells" it, and her suspicions are confirmed after Othello gives an account of the handkerchief. She incriminates her husband, who publicly kills her by stabbing her in the back. Dying, she wishes to be laid by the side of her mistress, for whom obviously her affection was much greater than for her husband. She dies in excruciating pathos, singing Desdemona's song of "Willow, willow, willow": "I will play the swan, / And die in music."

BRABANTIO

We meet Brabantio in the opening scene of the play. He and his household have been aroused by Roderigo and Iago. The latter pushes the panic button, shouting, "thieves, thieves." He describes the elopement of Brabantio's daughter in the lowest possible physical terms. We learn that Brabantio has definitely refused Roderigo for a son-in-law and does not want him to haunt his doors. Roderigo gives a fairly restrained account of what has happened. Brabantio calls for light and arouses his people. He is profoundly shocked: "O, she deceives me / Past thought!" He immediately thinks of the use of "charms," or love-philtres in which the Elizabethans believed. By these "the property of youth and maidhood / May be abus'd." He sets out to arrest Othello on charges of being a "practiser / Of arts inhibited and out of warrant." Othello cannot be arrested, because he has just been called to the Venetian senate on state business. Brabantio decides to press his charges before the senate.

Brabantio's major assumption is that the elopement errs "against all rules of nature." His case explodes, first because of the obvious sincerity and dignity of Othello, secondly because of the irrefutable evidence of Desdemona herself. The Duke advises Othello to "take up this mangled matter at the best."

Brabantio, while a man of strong prejudices, is open to reason, and has a great respect for law. He generously gives his daughter to Othello, at the same time frankly saying: "Which, but thou hast already, with all my heart / I would keep from thee." Brabantio's last lines in the scene (I, iii) seem to contradict his previous general impulse:

Look to her, Moor, if thou hast eyes to see: She has deceiv'd her father, and may thee.

The obvious explanation here is that Brabantio is doubling as "chorus" for the purpose of dramatic **foreshadowing**. It seems utterly out of place for him to doubt his own daughter's capacity for marital fidelity-if thou hast eyes to see.

We have two further references to Brabantio in the play. In Act IV, ii, the scene in which Othello treats Desdemona as if she was an inmate of a house of ill fame, Desdemona does not see the grave import of Othello's behavior. She feels that Othello is behaving in this way because of some worry over public business. Lodovico, the Venetian ambassador, had brought news that Othello had been recalled to Venice and that Cassio was to replace him. With this in mind, Desdemona says: "If haply you my father do suspect / An instrument of this your calling back, / Lay not your blame on me." There is no actual evidence in the play that Brabantio had anything to do with Othello's recall. The second reference is in a statement of Gratiano (V, ii). He says that he is glad that Desdemona's father is dead. The implication is that Brabantio has been spared the horrible news of Desdemona's death. Gratiano alleges that he had died from grief over Desdemona's marriage: "They match was mortal to him, and pure grief / Shore his old thread in twain . . ."

CASSIO

Cassio features importantly in the plot mechanism of the play, but he is comparatively unemphatic as a personality and as a dramatic character. He is more acted upon than acting. Basically he is a Venetian gentleman of the officer class, with a dedicated, though not fanatical, interest in his own career and advancement.

At the beginning of the play, Iago alleges that he is an untried officer, a mere theorist: "mere prattle, without practice, / Is all his soldiership." In the play he does not act very competently as an important officer. In his own words, he had "very poor and unhappy brains for drinking." Knowing that, he, however, allows himself to take that extra drop too much. He becomes intoxicated while on duty in a city under martial law. Iago, who has pre-arranged all the circumstances that are to lead to Cassio's disgrace, refers in this scene (II, iii) to Cassio as a soldier "fit to stand by Caesar / And give direction." He adds, of course, that his incapacity for drinking will someday lead to disaster. Othello had little choice but to dismiss Cassio on the spot from his command, for Cassio had been publicly drunk on duty.

Irony is piled on top of irony, for Cassio goes to Iago for consolation and advice. Iago tells him not to worry about his reputation-it's nothing! It is characteristic of the mediocre strain in Cassio that he is chiefly concerned with his reputation, not the danger to the city, or the embarrassment to the army. Iago argues that there are ways of regaining the general's good graces, that Cassio's punishment is more a matter of policy than of malice. He advises Cassio to plead through Desdemona: "Our general's wife is now the general . . ." "She is of so free, so kind, so apt, so blessed a disposition, she holds it a vice in her goodness not to do more than she is requested . . ."

Cassio, as a careerist, is punctilious about surface social forms. On the quay side in Cyprus he has exhibited the new fashionable etiquette by kissing Desdemona's hand. Iago resented this symbol of a higher social world: "With as little a web as this will I ensnare as great a fly as Cassio." Cassio has a "smooth dispose (appearance) . . . fram'd to make women false." "The knave is handsome, young . . ." We learn that Cassio was the go-between in Othello's wooing of Desdemona (III, iii), according to the special **conventions** of Renaissance courtship. Obviously Cassio had been selected for this service (before his appointment as second-in-command of the army) because of his special social training. Cassio is what the British would call "a nice chap." But he has no deep convictions, and his moral code is strictly limited to what men of his class did. He would not think of violating sexual morality in regard to a "lady" (Desdemona), but with regard to a woman of much inferior social status, the army courtesan, Bianca, his principles are of quite a different kind. His immediate implementation of Iago's advice ("the general's wife is now the general") is social to employ a band of musicians to play before the general's apartment on the morning after the consummation of the marriage. Othello is annoyed and pays them money to go away!

In his relationship to Desdemona it is assumed that, as soon as circumstances permit, Cassio will be reinstated in his army position. Desdemona says that Othello shall in "strangeness stand no further off / Than in politic distance." Cassio has a realistic view about his career. "Politic distance" may last far too long! Someone else may be temporarily appointed ("I being absent and my place supplied"), and such appointment might become permanent ("My general will forget my love and service"). We need not go into the details of how Desdemona, in her determined forthrightness and innocence, argues on behalf of Cassio. She has a distinctly feminine view, a deeply human view, and cannot understand the rational rigors of army discipline. Friends are friends, and what if wars must makes "examples" of people?

Desdemona insists on bringing the matter of Cassio to Othello's notice at the very time that he is so agitated by the disappearance of the handkerchief (III, iv). He leaves in a fury. Cassio appears on the scene immediately afterwards. Ironically, he is still pursuing his quiet careerist aims, totally unaware of the impending cyclone of the tragedy. In effect he wants to know where he stands. If Othello's answer is definitely no, he will seek some other career ("And shut myself up in some other course, / To fortune's alms").

It is not necessary to elaborate Cassio's relationship to Bianca in detail. We have discussed elsewhere the machinery whereby Iago is able to convey the impression to Othello (IV, i) that the dialogue between Iago and Cassio about Bianca is really about Desdemona. It is dramatically ironic, of course, that Cassio's immoral relationship with Bianca becomes an unconscious instrument for the destruction of Desdemona. It is this relationship to Bianca also that provides the opportunity for the attempt on Cassio's life in Aet V, Scene i.

At the end of the play, when the chain events set in motion by Iago is unravelled, Othello asks pardon of Cassio. After Othello's suicide, Cassio is left to rule in Cyprus.

RODERIGO

Roderigo has to be understood in terms of the tradition of "Courtly Love" - something quite outside normal American experience. We have commented on this in Act I, Scene i. We know that Roderigo had attempted to court Desdemona before she came to know Othello. Brabantio, Desdemona's father, would have none of it. Roderigo is so infatuated with Desdemona that he sincerely believes that he can come to some underhand arrangement with her. Even within the terms of Courtly Love we are meant to consider him a good deal of a fool. He is described in the Dramatis Personae as a "gulled" gentleman -"gull" is the rough Elizabethan slang equivalent of our term "sucker." And Iago, indeed, never "gives this sucker an even break."

While technically a "gentleman" (a man of "aristocratic" birth - "gentle" in this sense), Roderigo exhibits the lowest form of Venetian decadence. Iago takes money shamelessly from him ("Thus do I ever make my fool my purse") on the illusory promise of making the "arrangement." We learn in Act IV, Scene ii, that Roderigo has placed valuable jewels in the hands of Iago to be transferred to Desdemona for the purposes of seduction. Iago, of course, misappropriates the property.

From the point of view of dramatic structure, Roderigo serves the purpose of completely filling in the portrait of Iago. The long conversations between them bring into sharp focus Iago's underlying values and his skill in the manipulation of others. Roderigo wants to drown himself on learning of Desdemona's marriage, but Iago assures him, in his cynical way, that the marriage cannot last. It would be a "sport" to make a "cuckold" (i.e., deceived husband) out of Othello. Let Roderigo disguise his appearance and follow the couple to Cyprus.

In Cyprus, Iago persuades Roderigo to become the agent for Iago's plot to disgrace Cassio: He's rash and very sudden in choler, and haply may strike at you: provoke him, that he may;

for even out of that will I cause these of Cyprus to mutiny . . ." Roderigo does just that, with complete success.

Roderigo has quite a "disturbed" and inconsistent personality. When Iago had attempted to persuade him of a possible, even a probable, adultery between Cassio and Desdemona, Roderigo could not believe it: "I cannot believe that in her; she's full of most blessed condition." Yet, in spite of his high regard for Desdemona, he is aiming at a similar arrangement himself! We learn in Act V, ii, that the jewels he has entrusted to Iago to give to Desdemona "would half have corrupted a votarist." Roderigo is about to show some signs of manhood; he is no longer going to tolerate what he has "foolishly suffered" at the hands of Iago. But Iago winds him around his finger. Othello may leave for Mauretania, taking Desdemona with him. The only way to delay his departure is by the killing of Cassio. Roderigo is not immediately pliable to the proposition ("I will hear further reason for this"), but we have no doubt that Iago will "manipulate" him. Roderigo attempts to kill Cassio from ambush but bungles the assignment, and is himself wounded. He is then killed by Iago under the pretense of having stumbled on Cassio's "robbers." Iago wants to be sure that there will be no claim on the jewels that he has himself stolen, and he welcomes the removal of a potential witness. Roderigo had undertaken the projected murder in a completely detached way: "'Tis but a man gone." Robert Heilman comments on this line: "It does away with every value of imperative or speculation that 'man' or the death of man traditionally evokes, and it makes 'a man' simply a neutral instance of a category, a statistical item, an object that can be acted on without moral responsibility." If Cassio's mediocrity is concealed under a smooth social veneer, Roderigo is a "gentleman" decadent to the point of being a would-be adulterer, an ineffective practitioner of murder, and a complete fool. Even Iago has some admirable qualities compared to those of Roderigo's. The dramatic reason that we do not react to him with more contempt is that his role in the play is a very minor one, basically serving as a means of bringing Iago into focus.

BIANCA

While Bianca is a woman of loose morality, she seems, on her part, to be genuinely in love with Cassio. While she is listed as a "courtesan," her behavior is more like that of a "mistress." In Act III, iv, she has felt Cassio's absence deeply. His relationship to her is much more casual. He is somewhat embarrassed by it; he does not want Othello to see him in her company. Iago always gives the lowest possible estimate of people, and we have to make allowance for his perverse exaggeration. He describes Bianca (IV, 1) as "a housewife that by selling her desires / Buys herself bread and clothes . . ." He claims that when Cassio hears of her, he cannot restrain from "excess of laughter." Actually when Iago suggests that Cassio might marry her, Cassio does burst into laughter (the concealed Othello is led to believe that the reference is to Desdemona). Her "unconscious" role in the matter of the handkerchief has been previously dealt with. Cassio is attacked coming from an assignation at her lodgings. Iago, assuming that Cassio is dead, tries to implicate her in the presumed murder (V, i).

OFFICIAL FIGURES: DUKE OF VENICE, MONTANO, LODOVICO, GRATIANO

All these characters are in the background of the action. The Duke is a dignified and impartial judge, advising Brabantio to make the best of an established state of facts. Montano is the young governor of Cyprus, distinguished, as Othello says (II, iii), by "gravity" and "stillness"; his name is great "in mouths of wisest censure." He is wounded in the drunken brawl that disgraces Cassio. Lodovico is a kinsman of Brabantio, and Gratiano is Brabantio's brother. Lodovico acts as the Venetian ambassador in the recall of Othello to Venice (though later Iago says that Othello is going to Mauretania). He witnesses Othello's public striking of his wife. Along with Montano and Gratiano, he is present on stage in the last moments of Othello's life. He produces the letters proving the intrigues of Iago and Roderigo. Gratiano tells us that Brabantio died through grief over Desdemona's marriage.

OTHELLO

....

Othello is a tense, closely-knit play, with an ever-increasing emotional sweep. It is no less a great work of art than Hamlet, but it does not provide critics with as much material to talk about. Our own age is preoccupied with psychological analysis, and those works of art tend to be highly rated, perhaps overrated, which emphasize complex mental problems and deal with "ambiguity." Charles Dickens and Sir Walter Scott have receded to the wings of the theatre of literature, while the forestage is dominated by men like James Joyce and Franz Kafka. *Hamlet,* which presents a complicated "inward" personality, probably absorbs more than its share of Shakespeare criticism, while *Othello,* which emphasizes a noble but relatively uncomplicated personality, receives correspondingly less notice. Iago certainly should provide ample material for psychiatric study, but he has one obvious disadvantage from the point of view of attracting modern critical analysis. He is not representative of common modern psychic dilemmas in that way that *Hamlet* is. *Hamlet,* it could be argued, resembles many modern men, while Iago is an eccentric even in own time.

The earlier criticism of *Othello* did not examine details. We have quoted elsewhere Dr. Samuel Johnson's effective summary of the **theme** of the play (1765). Charles Lamb repeats one of his favorite ideas, that we are more understanding of a play, it possessing greater imaginative appeal, when we read it rather than when we see it acted. He objects to the stage presentation of a "coal-black Moor:" "The error of supposing that because Othello's color does not offend us in the reading, is should also not offend us in the seeing, is just such a fallacy as supposing that an Adam and Eve in a picture shall affect us just as they do in the poem." (1810). William Hazlitt, whom we have quoted elsewhere, is one of the first critics to be fascinated by the problem that the character of Iago presents. He argues that Iago's villainy is "without sufficient motive" (1817). In his "Notes on *Othello*" (1818?), Samuel Taylor Coleridge parallels the thought of Hazlitt in speaking of Iago's "motiveless malignity," and like Charles Lamb, Coleridge cannot accept Othello as a black man. In *Table Talk*, Dec. 20, 1822, he says that "Othello must not be conceived as a black man, but a high and chivalrous Moorish chief." Coleridge does not develop any unique thesis about the play, as he does in the case of Hamlet.

A much more penetrating criticism of *Othello* begins with A. C. Bradley's *Shakespearean Tragedy* (1904), in which the characters and their relationships are studied in detail. Bradley believes that Iago is entirely plausible, and that Othello is natural, simple and extroverted. But Bradley is not infallible, and many critics disagree with him. Lily B. Campbell in Shakespeare's *Tragic Heroes: Slaves of Passion* (1930) finds two main mistakes in Bradley's criticism: that he reads Shakespeare "assuming in his innocence that the words and scenes mean what they seem to mean," and that he accepted the persons of the plays as real men and women. "Bradley is forever busy," she says, "with his paint brush, filling in what is not there in Shakespeare's portraits, and worse, altering what is there." Miss Campbell herself throws some interesting light on *Othello* in terms of historical scholarship. She analyzes the views of jealousy in Shakespearean times. She makes an interesting point about Othello's unbookish jealousy. Iago says (IV, i, 101ff): As he shall smile, Othello shall go mad; And his unbookish jealousy must construe Poor Cassio's smiles, gestures, and light behaviors Quite in the wrong.

If *Othello* had read more widely in Elizabethan psychology, if he had not been so unbookish, he would have been able to see that the words and gestures of Cassio could not possibly have meant what Othello thought they meant.

A great deal of the most brilliant Shakespeare criticism belongs to our own era. Several works deserve special notice. Other critical works are more conveniently reviewed according to the topics they discuss. The first is Robert B. Heilman's magic in the *Web: Action and Language in Othello* (1956). This is an extremely sensitive application of the new criticism, in which the total effect of the work is kept constantly in mind, and the role of images and their interrelationships are studied in terms of their ultimate united impact. The explorations are not confined simply to poetry, but search deeply into the philosophical and religious values of the work. Like his previous work on *King Lear* (*This Great Stage: Image and Structure in King Lear*), Dr. Heilman's book on *Othello* enables the student to see Shakespeare's stature in an entirely new dimension. The second noteworthy book on *Othello* is Marvin Rosenberg's *The Masks of Othello* (1961). This book offers many incidental insights into the art and poetry of the play, but it is primarily a study of the stage history of the work through the various centuries. This history is a great aid to the proper interpretation of the play, for staging purposes, which, if followed, will prevent the resistance to the play, with which audience through the ages have met "faddy" or "far-out" renditions.

Another especially important work, particularly in regard to a specific commentary on the text of Othello, is G. R. Elliott's *Flaming Minister* (1953). The book, named from a line in Act V, Scene ii, in which Othello refers to the candle flickering by Desdemona's bedside, offers the theory, previously noted, that the tragic flaw in *Othello* is a deficiency in the quality of his love.

Innumerable problems concerning *Othello* have caught the attention of critics both early and modern. Several problems of special interest are discussed on the following pages.

CONSTRUCTION

Othello has been highly praised for its technical construction. G. B. Harrison says that it is "the best constructed of all Shakespeare's tragedies," repeating A. C. Bradley (*Shakespearean Tragedy*) to the effect that it is the most "masterly." There is a cohesiveness, a compactness, in Othello which are unusual in Shakespeare's plays. There is, for example, no sub-plot-our concern is entirely with the fate of Othello and Desdemona. The one comic scene (III, i, 1-31) is usually cut in modern performance (probably because it is not very funny). The action commences from the first scene and our interest is never surfeited. Othello stands in the center of the tragedy, perhaps not always as interesting a character as Iago, but exciting our sympathy far more. Dr. Johnson has remarked that little or nothing is wanting to render Othello a "regular" tragedy (by that, Dr. Johnson meant a neo-classical play, strictly according to the book). The only requirement would be to have the play open with Othello's arrival at Cyprus, and the matter of the preceding act rendered through expository narration. Coleridge discusses this question, whether or not such a change would have been an improvement. Coleridge maintains that it is a rather foolish question because all rules are a means to an end, and that *Othello* attains artistic unity.

Objections have arisen to the plausibility of the plot. A leading iconoclast in this respect was the eighteenth century neo-classical critic, Rymer, who referred to the play as the "bloody tragical farce of the dropped handkerchief." The point is that construction of a work of art and its plausibility can be viewed on various levels, some important and essential, other comparatively trivial and even irrelevant. Elmer Edgar Stoll maintains that the plausibility we have a right to expect in a play is in terms of the actual acting out of the dramatic "illusion" on the stage. If we do not see any lack of plausibility in the play as it is performed and comes to life before us, then for artistic purposes there is no lack of plausibility. What may eventuate in a detailed study in a library, Stoll feels, is something quite different. Any Shakespearean play, minutely studied in this way, reveals not only implausibilities but also outright inconsistencies. The appendices to A. C. Bradley's *Shakespearean Tragedy* reveal quite a few, and more recent research swells the number. The machinery of the "dropped handkerchief" in Othello would be viewed, according to the Stoll point of view, as an indication that Othello sought for real evidence, and did not rely on the word of Iago alone. Its plausibility would have to be judged as a stage device within the terms of an acted drama. Whether it could bear sifting and cross-examinations in a court of law would be quite a different matter.

PATHOS

One critic states that "a great tragedy depends upon the artist's ability to express the moral sense representing the universal experience of man." To quote G. B. Harrison in *Shakespeare's Tragedies*, "True tragedy exists only when it produces in the spectator a definite emotional reaction. . . . The first gift essential to the tragic dramatist is a profound moral sense, for unless he has his own instinctive sense of joy and sorrow, of pity and terror, of right and wrong, good and evil, he is incapable of being moved and moving."

Many critics have held that, in abundance of tragic feeling and pathos, Othello stands highest among Shakespeare's tragedies. William Hazlitt, A. C. Bradley and E. K. Chambers, for example, think that *Othello,* more than any other of Shakespeare's plays, produces that tragic pity which the Greeks thought essential to tragedy. A. C. Bradley declares, "Of all Shakespeare's tragedies, not even excepting *King Lear, Othello* is the most painfully exciting and the most terrible. From the moment when the temptation begins, the reader's heart and mind are held in a vice, experiencing the extremes of pity and fear, sympathy and repulsion, sickening hope and dreadful expectation."

THE TRAGIC THEME OF OTHELLO

Shakespeare's tragedies are normally characterized by a "prodominant" hero, a tradition that began with the theater of Christopher Marlowe. The dominance of *Othello* is somewhat obscured at first, because it is Iago who initiates the course of tragic action, but, in terms of moral stature, ultimate decision, and emotional crisis, Othello himself is at the center of the picture. As F. R. Leavis states, "*Othello* is the chief personage in such a sense that the tragedy may be said to be Othello's character in action. Iago is subordinate and merely ancillary." The dominance of the tragic hero correlates with a dominant **theme** in a tragedy, a tradition going back in varying ways to the medieval morality plays.

"Jealousy" is the **theme** almost universally associated with *Othello*. But the word had two meanings in Shakespeare's day and in the tragedy itself. Frequently the word means "suspicion." In *Othello* it has this meaning at least as often as that of "sexual jealousy." Othello tells us that he is not the sort of man to "make a life of jealousy," following the changes of the moon with fresh suspicions. "Jealousy," in the sense of a possessive love which will not even tolerate the idea of a competitor, creates unfounded suspicion. In Othello's case, suspicion is not unfounded but is created first by a master of the craft, Iago, before there is any question of sexual jealousy.

OTHELLO'S "JEALOUSY"

But the question of Othello's jealousy, how to define it and evaluate it, has been a constant subject of debate among the leading Shakespearean critics. They seem to divide into two groups. The first group, among which are included Lily B. Campbell and Harley Granville-Barker, claims that it was the passion of sexual jealousy which led to the fall of Othello; while other authorities, influenced chiefly by A. C. Bradley, maintain that Shakespeare's *Othello* was not inclined to sexual jealousy; but rather it was his openness to deception which constituted his "tragic flaw." A. C. Bradley states, "His tragedy lies in this, that his whole nature was indisposed to jealousy, and yet was such that he was unusually open to deception, and, if once wrought to passion, likely to act with little reflection, with no delays and in the most decisive manner conceivable." From a close study of Othello's character, one could easily see that Othello was not basically jealous; yet to state that his openness to deception was his tragic flaw would seem to over-simplify the matter. G. R. Elliott in *Flaming Minister* emphasizes self-esteem and pride as contributing factors-in Othello's case, of deceit working on pride. Such differences of opinion lead to a consideration of the quality of Othello's love for Desdemona. Elliott, in another context, argues that Shakespeare is insistent on exhibiting the weakness of Othello's spiritual sentiments in the face of his "selfish" passion. F. R. Leavis argues these doubts about the "unselfishness" of Othello's love as follows: "Iago, like Bradley, points out that Othello didn't really know Desdemona, and Othello acquiesces in considering her a type-a type outside his experience - the Venetian wife. It is plain, then, that his love is composed very largely of ignorance of self as well as of her: however nobly he may feel about it, it isn't altogether what he, and Bradley with him, thinks it is. It may be love, but it can only be an oddly qualified sense love of her: it must be much more a matter of self-centered and self-regarding satisfaction-pride and sensual possessiveness, appetite, love of loving, than he suspects." As we summarize the various scenes in the play, light will be thrown on these disputed issues.

Jealousy, in the form of envy, is reinforced in the play by Roderigo's hostility to Othello's possession of Desdemona, and by Iago's general maliciousness toward Othello's "free and open nature."

SLAVE OF PASSION?

Lily B. Campbell has popularized the image of Shakespeare's tragic heroes as slaves of passion. Mark Van Doren characterized Othello as a man who is continuously warring with his suppressed, "barbarian" nature. Othello is the military commander-in-chief of a state that was at the time a world power, and, in the play, he is held in respect, and even in awe, by nearly all. He is distinguished by a public image of self-control, dignity, decision. In some ways, he is a social stranger to Venice (and Iago capitalizes on this fact), but it would seem that he is "exotic" rather than "barbaric." In regard to the "slave of passion" thesis, an analogy can be made between *Othello* and *King Lear.*

Both Othello and King Lear are similar in that they both were blinded to the truth by their own self-pity. And each was confronted with a situation which each had in his power to control, but neither was humble enough to realize the truth. Both were slaves to passion-Othello to sexual jealousy and King Lear to wrath. Neither sought to find the truth, but acted in his hurt. The punishment both inflicted on their loved one did not fit the crime, for Desdemona and Cordelia were innocent of any crime. The crime was only in the mind of each of the punishers. Both men died regretting the wrong they had done.

THE FALL FROM HIGH ESTATE

A constant **theme** of medieval literature was the fall of the hero from high estate. The contrast between the hero's apparent security and the sudden disaster that overtook him was considered the essence of tragedy. Aristotle's subtlety about the "tragic flaw" was not generally considered. This medieval **theme**, of course, is also present in *Othello.* William McCollom feels that "the chief reason the hero must be superior to most men is that otherwise he cannot awaken that intense concern for man's plight which is certainly essential to tragedy." The tragic hero faces, on a more exalted level, the dilemmas of ordinary men, and "his fall will therefore have a greater resonance than that of most men." *Othello,* on the face of things, presents a fall that would appear as unlikely as that of a tower.

APPEARANCE VERSUS REALITY

Theodore Spencer in *Shakespeare and the Nature of Man* argues that a traditional sense of unity, entering many orders (cosmological, natural, political), had been disturbed in Shakespeare's time by many new lines of thought and by some notable scientific discoveries, especially in the field of astronomy. Doubt had been placed upon the belief in the nobility and dignity of man. The violation of this sense of order, of this sense of unity, "was being felt everywhere at the end of the sixteenth century, and it was a violation which, when it occurred in any one part, was felt throughout the whole structure. It was because Shakespeare, as he produced his art, was able to see individual experience in relation to the all-inclusive conflict produced by this violation, that his great tragedies have such wide reverberations and give us so profound a picture of the nature of man." Appearance and reality could not any longer be equated, and Spencer finds the **theme** of the conflict between appearance and reality basic to Shakespearean tragedy. True good and "seeming good" may be poles apart, and the universe is full of potential deception. "Men should be what they seem, or else might they seem none," Othello observes, unaware of his own position relative to that of Iago.

IAGO, MAN OF APPEARANCE

This difference between appearance and reality is not just an aspect of the Iago-Othello relationship, but it is the essence of the entire tragedy. Othello is deceived by appearances, and judges Iago to be honest and Desdemona false. He feels that his is administering justice when actually he is murdering an innocent, spotless woman. Theodore Spencer has pointed out that Iago not only exemplifies the concept of the difference between outer show and inner fact, but also the concept of the evil man as the incomplete man, a man who represents the Renaissance type of the man "whose reason controls his passions and yet he is wholly bad." Iago has no lust to link him with animals, and he has no capacity for seeing himself in relation to state or the universal order of things. He is an unscrupulous individualist possessed by mysterious drives. "Virtue! A fig! 'Tis in ourselves that we are thus or thus."

Capable of the malevolence and treachery of a Borgia or Sforza, he assumes the blunt outspokenness of the soldier to convince Othello of his honesty. He disguises his intentions perfectly, and his cleverness and hypocrisy enable him to manipulate Othello and arouse in him his fatal suspicions. In one of his earliest speeches, where he is revealing himself to Roderigo and the audience, he describes himself as a thoroughgoing egoist, rejecting the obsolete tradition of service and fidelity:

. . .Other there are Who, trimmed in forms and visages of duty, Keep yet their hearts attending on themselves; And, throwing but shows of service on their lords, Do well thrive by them, and when they have lined their coats, Do themselves homage. These fellows have some soul; And such a one do I profess myself.

Then he says that the outward appearance he gives to the world bears no relation to the reality inside: "I am not what I am."

IAGO AS MACHIAVELLIAN

The adjective "Machiavellian" has been repeatedly applied to Iago, but it is an epithet that only applies very roughly. Machiavelli in the Prince had in mind public and political morality rather than the ethics of a private citizen. A prince can do certain things for the benefit or defense of the state that would not be permissible to anyone in a private capacity. And Machiavelli was careful to add that a prince should act decently whenever he could and whenever such action would not conflict with his self-interest. "Thus it is well to seem merciful, faithful, humane, sincere, religious, and also to be so: but you must have the mind so disposed that when it is needful to be otherwise you may be able to change to the opposite qualities. And it must be understood that a prince, especially a new prince, cannot observe all those things which are considered good in men, being often obliged, in order to maintain the state, to act against faith, against charity, against humanity, and against religion." In so far as Machiavelli encouraged the image of the man of virtu ("these fellow have some soul"), Iago may be considered in this tradition. The man of virtue is not a man of virtue, but a man who knows what he wants (almost exclusively in terms of power), and goes after it by the shortest and most effective route. Virtu indicates amoral courage, independence, daring. But even the man of virtu acts morally if this serves his purpose. In Iago we have other dimensions. First of all, he is not a political person acting for political ends. Secondly, he does not conduct his intrigue successfully in attaining the objective he said he had in mind (he actually gives us several objectives which would not fit into any Machiavellian program.) He does not gain Cassio's post, and the intrigue, as several critics see it, gets completely out of hand and out of his control.

Mr. G. R. Elliott takes the view that Iago's plan overshot the mark and that he did not foresee the violence of Othello's reaction to the alleged infidelity of Desdemona. "But the fact is that this character is imperfectly drawn. Not all the efforts of his admiring interpreters have succeeded in divesting him of a certain air of staginess. Their subtle lucubrations upon his so-called "motive-hunting" have helped to demonstrate that he is not coherently motivated. . . . His two roles, smart buffoon and 'heavy villain' are not well harmonized." From a Machiavellian point of view, Iago looks much smarter on the surface than he really is. Some mania, some neurosis, seems to have a hold on him that is unsuitable for the cool calculations of a Machiavellian.

IS IAGO PLAUSIBLE?

A wide variety of questions have been asked about Iago. Is he a plausible character, and, if so, is he understandable in human terms or is he to be regarded as some sort of diabolical symbol? A position taken by Elmer Edgar Stoll is that we should simply regard him a "good" villain-not good, of course, in a moral sense, but in an artistic one. Tragedy is an art of conflict, and, since good does not conflict with good (beyond the point of a temporary misunderstanding), in order to stimulate the requisite excitement in a drama, an effective villain is aesthetically necessary. In this sense, an audience enjoys a "good" villain; he starts "the ball rolling." Stoll accepts Iago as an "initial postulate for a greater dramatic effect," an effect of simplification and concentration. "It is a mechanical device, to be sure, this intrusion of the villain; but there is something of the mechanical in most art, once we get to the bottom of it. It is in a fugue and in a symphony and of much the same sort in a great fugue or symphony as in a mediocre work. This difference of quality lies not in the contrivance itself but in the use of it, in what is thereby contrived."

IAGO'S SATANISM

Stoll's view renders arguments for Iago's plausibility unnecessary. So does the view which would make Iago a diabolic symbol. As one critic says: "And Iago's motives? They have always been a problem. Surely his very possession of this spiritual, flame-like, Mephistophelean intelligence is Shakespeare's reason for the absence of apparent motive; the utterly diabolical do not need motives for their evil acts, and a demi-devil needs no motive beyond the pleasure of employing the most exquisite machine, his mind, proving to himself the worthlessness of love and ideals and romance." Some support for this view can be found in Othello's own conclusions about Iago, which are unconcerned with analysis-Iago is simply the devil (V, 11): "If that thou be'st a devil, I cannot kill thee," and "Will you, I pray, demand that demi-devil / Why he has thus ensnar'd my soul and body?"

An extension of this view is to view *Othello* as a medieval religious drama. This is the point of view of Paul Siegel in *The Damnation of Othello.* Just as Adam before him, Othello questions his earthly paradise, and again like Adam before him, loses it through an act of his own will. Othello's destruction serves as a notice to all that no man is invulnerable to the destructive power of evil. "The moment of his kneeling to vow vengeance is the moment of Othello's giving himself over to Iago. . . . He kneels side by side with Othello, and vows to be in his service. The oaths that the two exchange are as awful in their solemnity as the Faustus oath. It is a pact with the devil that Othello has made. Iago becomes Othello's Mephistopheles and in making the devil his servant Othello gives himself up into his power."

IAGO, A METAPHYSICAL PROBLEM

Ultimately in regard to Iago we have a **"metaphysical"** problem, since in dealing with him we have to deal with the first principles of good and evil. Normally our Western tradition on this subject derives from Greek philosophy. Like Socrates in Plato's dialogues, we tend to think that, if a man sees and understands the good, he cannot choose but to follow the good. And, even if a man pursues evil, we tend to think that it is due to lack of knowledge. In seeking evil, he is following a "mistaken good." It is almost impossible for us to accept the image of a man who loves evil for its own sake, knowing full well what it is, and who, conversely, hates the good because it is good. But Iago forces us to reconsider these problems. Such malice may not develop overnight, but a career of deceit, frustration, and hatred might bring a man to such a point. J. I. M. Stewart says of Iago that the hatred which he embodies springs from within him. Iago seen in this context is a concentration of destructive hatred whose aim is to destroy whatever is good in its environment. Shakespeare underlines the **theme** that Iago particularly enjoys destroying people through their good qualities. Anyone can destroy another through his weaknesses. The challenge is to destroy him through his strengths. Iago says in regard to Desdemona, "So will I turn her virtue into pitch, / And out of her own goodness make the net / That shall enmesh them all." Granted, of course, that such iniquity is possible, the next question that arises is: is such a man sane? If we define a man who pursues evil for its own sake as insane, the problem of moral responsibility is bypassed. And the question of an adequate definition of clinical insanity in such a situation is very difficult. Iago does not appear insane, at least in dramatic terms. But there is no doubt that he is "sick," though his intelligence is always alert. Modern psychiatry, of course, recognizes this situation in which the surface mind works with maximum efficiency, while the world of emotion and the world of conscience may have been reduced to zero.

LOCAL COLOR

Dr. Robert Heilman has contrasted the "dark" and "light" **imagery** that runs thematically through *Othello*. Othello, as A. C. Bradley has pointed out, is probably a black man, as is abundantly suggested by the text. He is not a "Moor" in the modern usage of the word; he is not Arab and Mohammedan, but black and Christian. Venice, which was a leading power in Othello's day and, as we would say, the "great free port" of the Mediterranean, safeguarded the rights of all minorities, whether Mohammedan or Jewish (compare Shylock's basic position in the same city), whether Christian or pagan. This tolerance and international atmosphere constituted one of the main reasons for the success of Venice, in addition to its strategic geographical location. International merchants knew that, whatever their background, their rights were guaranteed in law and their contracts would be enforced. Venice does not hesitate to place an outstanding black general like Othello in command of its armies. His marriage to Desdemona is viewed primarily as "romantic" rather than as a "racial problem," though certain aspects of the latter are not overlooked by Iago and Brabantio. Othello is not a "problem" play as a similar situation would be in modern American drama. In fact, many students become immersed in this tense play without being aware that there is any racial problem at all. It receives minor emphasis and is "peripheral" to the course of the tragedy as a whole. In regard to Othello's color, A. C. Bradley comments that "in regard to the essentials of his character it [Othello's race] is not important; and if anyone had told Shakespeare that no Englishman would have acted like the Moor, and had congratulated him on the accuracy of his racial psychology, I am sure he would have laughed." But Iago, in contrast to other characters in the play, does pass disparaging remarks about Othello: 'old black ram,' 'Barbary horse,' 'erring barbarian.'"

Shakespeare shows himself so well acquainted not only with the customs but with the physical landmarks of Venice, as to give rise to the conjecture that he may have spent some of the "lost years" of his biography in Italy and in this city. As in *The Merchant of Venice*, which has the same setting, Shakespeare makes references which would be difficult to learn second-hand from a traveler or from maps, however detailed. *The Sagitary in Othello* (I, 1, 159) was commonly thought to be an inn, although it is not mentioned by any travelers. Its name is a reference to a statue of Mars with bow and arrow that probably graced the official residence of the commanders of the galleys. In *The Merchant of Venice* Shakespeare estimates the distance between Monte Bello and Padua at twenty miles. It is. He also mentions a "traject" or ferry over the river Brenta between Padua and Venice. It actually existed. In *The Two Gentlemen of Verona* he mentions a fountain in Verona which has subsequently been excavated in the spot where Shakespeare said it was. There may be other explanations for the exactitude of such local references besides personal experience, but obviously, in his Italian plays, Shakespeare's local color has a reportorial quality.

OTHELLO

. . . .

Question: Did Iago have a goal?

Answer: Iago is a type of neurotic personality who is extremely cool and self-possessed on the surface, but concealed underneath are volcanoes of rage and resentment. In the contemporary world where there have been startling advancements in psychiatry and psychoanalysis, a certain amount of successful prodding can be made into such a personality. At least some causes can be assigned for some aspects of such a character. Few modern critics are co tent simply to summarize Iago's character as motiveless malignity.

On the other hand, even allowing for our greater subtlety today in mental analysis, we tend to pursue a mare's-nest if we strain to find reasons for the irrational. When we think of human goals, we think of reasonable human goals. It is almost impossible for us to think of destructiveness, self-hatred, sadism, as goals. Iago does not understand, or attempt to understand, his own urges; he just wants to make the world pay for his own interior tensions and frustrations. He enjoys his own operative skills, and more or less "struts" in his soliloquies, taking the audience into his unhappy plans and fantasies, confidentially letting them know how he can manipulate people and make monkeys out of them. But he never has enough insight into himself to wonder why he wants to make monkeys out of people. He makes wild stabs at rationality-Othello has had an affair with Emilia; so has Cassio. These ideas come upon Iago accidentally, casually; he does not pursue them. They have had no bearing on his own relations with Emilia. He has no objection to her continuing to work in Othello's household. What may conceivably pass for human reasons for his hostility-Emilia's infidelity, his being passed over for promotion in the army-he mentions once and then forgets. He becomes much more interested in destroying Othello than in managing a well-planned intrigue to assure his own advancement. He tells us that in following the Moor, he is following but himself. But where is he leading himself?

He views without alarm the idea that man is essentially corrupt, and, on the other hand, inconsistently claims that man's will and reason are the key to man's behavior (I, iii). Yet he gets no satisfaction from exercising will and reason. He is basically looking for emotion-charged situations that will satisfy his own irrational emotion of hatred. He wants to turn Desdemona's goodness into pitch. But he does not seem to know why he wants to do this anymore than a boy who smashes windows in an empty house or throws paint on public works of art. Obviously he enjoys torturing people psychologically, but how does this relate to advancement in the army or the fantasies of Emilia's adulteries? His stealing of Roderigo's jewels (IV, ii) and his subsequent murder of him make a certain amount of criminal sense, but these deeds are improvised and do not connect with any over-all goal. He wants to drive Othello "mad" (II, i), but the killing of Desdemona, at least at first, does not seem to be something he anticipated: "I am to pray you not to strain my speech / To grosser issues nor to larger reach /

Than to suspicion" (III, iii). He likes to connect himself with the "Divinity of hell!" (II, iii); he wants to "enmesh" them all.

Would one judge from all this that Iago is a cool and clever planner, or, in modern slang, is he "wild" and "mixed-up"? He has no goal in terms of any accepted scale of values. He does not think things "through" in an organized way; he improvises in response to his own disordered psychological pressures, though in his responses he is a brilliant tactician. The main advantage that Iago possesses is that no one is able to suspect him. He is the villain that everyone trusts. Iago ironically comments on his own situation in an exchange with Emilia after the terrifying scene in which Othello has treated Desdemona as the inmate of a house of ill fame (IV, ii):

Emil.

I will be hang'd, if some eternal villain, Some busy and insinuating rogue, Some cogging, cozening slave, to get some office, Have not devis'd this slander; I'll be hang'd else.

Iago.

Fie, there is no such man; it is impossible.

Iago's "Fie, there is no such man; it is impossible," illustrates that Iago relies on the fact that no one will believe that a human being can be as corrupt as himself. "The belief in the impossibility of utter turpitude is the very condition of Iago's existence." If we can say that destructiveness is successful, Iago is successful. It does violence to language, however, to describe destructiveness as a goal. Cleverness, however, is only one element in Iago's "success." He needed the aid of moral weaknesses in other characters-Desdemona's "white" lies,

Cassio's immoral relationship with Bianca, Emilia's failure to say where the handkerchief was. He also needed a great deal of pure "luck" - the right circumstance falling at the right time.

Question: What is meant by the word "nature" in *Othello*?

Answer: In a very generalized sense the word "nature" means "what makes a thing what it is." While nearly everyone is agreed on that point, a wide variety of views springs into being as to just "what makes." Three helpful books on the uses of the word "nature" in the Renaissance are those of Theodore Spencer, *Shakespeare and the Nature of Man*; E. M. W. Tillyard, *The Elizabethan World Picture*; and Hiram Haydn, *The Counter-Renaissance*.

The nature of man in terms of the great Renaissance humanist ideal is described succinctly in the words of Hamlet: "What a piece of work is a man! how noble in reason! how infinite in faculty! in from and moving how express and admirable! in action how like an angel! in apprehension how like a god! the beauty of the world! the paragon of animals!" That is the ideal, but the actual condition of men is somewhat different. Even Hamlet sets it down in his notebook, in reference to Cladius, "that one may smile, and smile, and be a villain." The ideal man thought in terms of certain Greek classical traditions; he conceived of the universe as a great cosmic harmony, all the spheres joining in one great orchestration of joy and power. This great world (the macrocosm) was reflected in the lesser world of man (the microcosm). All aspects of creation "correspond" (that is, harmoniously "answered") with one another in terms of a settled order and hierarchy. All creation would be happy if each being observed his proper function in the "Great Chain of Being." Once this chain is broken, as is observed in Troilus and Cressida, "Then everything includes itself in power, / Power into will, will into appetite." Appetite, aided by will and power, becomes a universal wolf, at last eating up itself.

The tension between the ideal and the actual state of facts, between what could be and what is, is at the heart of the great Shakespearean tragedies. In effect, what Shakespeare says about the nature of man is that the ideal can be realized (it is not something purely theoretical) in such persons as Hamlet, Othello, Desdemona, though they remain vulnerable. On the other hand, mankind has another dimension as revealed in the natures of Claudius and Iago, where appetite, in terms of will and power, has become a universal wolf.

It is the nature of man to yearn toward Heaven and to pursue the Good. In human terms, the good meant friendliness, forthrightness and service. Among Shakespeare's villains, Iago is unique in that he does not think of the good life at all; he has no traces of an operating conscience as have both Claudius and Macbeth. Sinful Macbeth recognizes the virtues he has sacrificed in the pursuit of power "as honor, love, obedience, troops of friends." Iago assumes that human nature is basically rotten ("the blood and baseness of our natures"), that so-called virtue is a hypocritical "cover-up" for essential vice. He believes love is just a fancy name for lust; people are driven and motivated by their vicious urges ("her eye must be fed"). Iago's reality is vice; "appearance" is virtue. Iago says of Othello, "The Moor is of a free and open nature." This is not a compliment, for Iago believes such a nature is unreal "that thinks men honest that but seem to be so." Iago is completely "unnatural"; he is the complete anti-humanist, the universal wolf driven on by will and power ("Our bodies are our gardens, to which our wills are gardeners").

It was one of the convictions of Renaissance humanists that the nature of essential qualities of goodness were love, outgoingness and creativity. The famous Italian humanist Baldassare Castiglione in the *Book of the Courtier* compared goodness to a reservoir of water, which is constantly flowing outwards, yet is always full and never diminishes its own being. This goodness in man is responsive to the beauty of all created things. Castiglione assumed that it is the "nature" of man to be attracted to the highest "sovereign" beauty and goodness which exist eternally. Such was the concept of ideal nature in Renaissance England. Men who deviated from these ideals were "unnatural," were examples of corrupted nature.

Shakespeare presents a view of corrupted "nature" in Iago, the unresponsive, negative, sterile man. Instead of being inspired toward Goodness by the beauty of women, in line with Renaissance humanist tradition, he is cold and detached, and expresses contempt both of women and sex. As Shakespeare sees it, man has free will. It is at least partly within "man's nature" to frame his own nature. Within broad limitations, a man makes himself by his desires, decisions, reactions from moment to moment. Shakespeare recognizes the image of man as it should be; but there he also notes the fact that man is too often what he should not be. Ironically, Shakespeare has Iago express this view when he says, "The power and corrigible authority of this lies in our wills."

One special use of the word "nature" should be noted in *Othello*. Brabantio argues that Desdemona's love for Othello errs "against all rules of nature." Later Iago repeats the same point in more detail (III, iii):

Not to affect many proposed matches Of her own clime, complexion, and degree, Whereto we see in all things nature tends - Foh! one may smell in such a will most rank, Foul disproportion, thoughts unnatural.

Brabantio and Iago here refer to a humanist code of behavior, such as Castiglione had prescribed, in which persons of a given rank, appearance, education, and sex were expected to conduct themselves with decorum, in accordance with the rules drawn up for that class. Thus, fair Desdemona, daughter of a noble Venetian, behaved "unnaturally" by failing to consult her father when she chose her own husband, and by eloping with the black Moor, a man who was outside her class and race. Shakespeare argues here for a different sort of "nature," not one based on humanist "rules" but on human passions. A strong mental and spiritual affinity exists between Desdemona and Othello ("I saw Othello's visage in his mind"). Dramatically, their affinities are the stronger for being accompanied by so much unlikeness in their physical appearance and social positions; the inward correspondence stands the more approved for the outward diversity.

Question: How is *Othello* dramatically constructed?

Answer: The traditional divisions of a drama are **exposition**, rising action, **climax**, falling action, and the conclusion or denouement.

Exposition:

The **exposition** has to identify the characters and sketch at least their general relationships to one another. Wherever possible, the characters should be shown performing acts significant of their personalities; they should be shown in action rather than be described. Shakespeare generally moves swiftly. In the opening scene, Shakespeare establishes the dissatisfaction of Iago and the fact of Othello's elopement, and then we are placed in the midst of action-Iago and Roderigo awakening the Brabantio household. In I, ii, a fight is imminent between the Brabantio and Othello forces, which Othello is able to prevent from going further by his dignity and diplomacy. We also witness the double-dealing of Iago; no one has to inform us about his capacity for dangerous deception. We see it! In I, iii, we have the great senate scene which establishes the relationship of Othello and Desdemona to one another and which enables Othello to recite his romantic autobiography at length-but still within the terms of the dramatic action. At the end of the scene in the long prose conversation between Iago and Roderigo, the conditions of the main conflict to come are established. Roderigo hopes to form an immoral relationship with Desdemona through the agency of Iago. Iago assures him that the marriage cannot last. In a soliloquy, Iago tells us that he plans to ruin Cassio, by leading Othello to think that Cassio is "too familiar with his wife." Cassio, the man who got the appointment that Iago was seeking, appeared briefly in I, ii, largely for the purpose of expositor identification.

The Rising Action:

The rising action implies complication and growing conflict. The characters, who have been identified in the **exposition** and who, at least in this play, have already been engaged in conflicts but not in the conflict, now become involved with one another and lay the groundwork of the major conflict. In II, i, we witness two separate arrivals in Cyprus from Venice: first, that of Desdemona, Iaga, Roderigo, and Emilia; second, that of Othello himself. Iago is preparing to make something of Cassio's exercising the new Venetian courtesy of hand-kissing. Desdemona and Othello greet one another for one moment of supreme happiness, but Iago stands to one side declaring: "O, you are well tun'd now! / But I'll set down the pegs that make this music, / As honest as I am." Iago, in a long passage with Roderigo, confides his plan of removing Roderigo's supposed rival corrupter, Cassio, by provoking some action that will put Cassio in a bad light. In II, iii, this plan is carried out. Cassio is induced to drink too much; Roderigo provokes him to a fight. Othello dismisses Cassio on the spot from his command. After Cassio's disgrace, Iago advises him to plead to Othello through Desdemona. In a soliloquy, Iago reveals his major design - to convince the Moor that Desdemona's intercession for Cassio is due to an adulterous relationship with him. The rising action is now drawing near to the **climax**. Iago is excited by his destructive ideas: "Pleasure and action make the hours seem short."

The Climax:

The **climax** always occurs in the third act of a Shakespearean play. Aristotle in the *Poetics* used a Greek word for the **climax** meaning "the tying of the knot." He thinks of the **exposition** as consisting in laying out the various threads of the story; the rising action presents the criss-crossing of these various threads; the **climax** shows the point where these threads are most tightly tied together. The **climax** is the point of highest tension where the conflict is totally joined, and where the suspense of the audience is greatest. "Whatever is going to happen in this situation, whatever is going to result from it?" the audience asks itself. The **climax** might be said to contain a series of climaxes within itself. - like a series of Chinese boxes, each one being removed soars to reach the innermost one. The first two scenes of Act III are merely informative. The **climax** of the play lies in III, iii. This is a very long scene of nearly 480 lines. This has been analyzed in detail elsewhere. Iago is able to "psychologize" Othello into suspicion without overtly saying anything. The birth of suspicion within Othello's own mind might well be considered the **climax** within the climax. Iago marks it with his incantation: "O beware, my lord, of jealousy; / It is the green-eyed monster which doth mock / The meat is feeds on. . . ." Othello is torn by his love of Desdemona and his long standing trust in Iago. He sees Desdemona for a brief moment, and we feel for an instant that Othello may escape Iago's temptation. But Iago begins to present alleged evidence about the handkerchief, which Emilia had just given to him, and about things Cassio was alleged to have said in his sleep. Othello seems convinced for the time, and he and Iago kneel together to swear revenge.

The Falling Action:

The falling action presents the consequences already implicit in the **climax**. Every dramatist has a difficult problem artistically after the climax. The **climax** is the point of highest tension, and the dramatist is subsequently in danger of weakening and diluting too much the tension he has created. He had to avoid "anti-climax" by introducing new sources of interest into the drama. Shakespeare's traditional method in tragedy is to raise the possibility that the hero or "**protagonist**" may find means of escaping the fate that is overtaking him. While Shakespeare does not say so in so many words, he shows us dramatically that Othello has had some second thoughts after the crisis in III, iii. He is looking into the "exsufflicate and blown surmises" matching Iago's "inference." He may not be doing this very effectively, because Iago is already exercising a very effective psychological domination over him. But at least he tries and this gives the audience some hope that the **protagonist** may yet pull out of his troubles. In III, iv, he asks Desdemona for the handkerchief. If she could have produced it, Othello's suspicions might well have ceased. From then on, the curve of Othello's fortunes turns downwards, but obviously he is still seeking what seems to him to be sure evidence. Iago arranges, in IV, 1, a sequence which seems to amount to Cassio's confession of guilt. At the end, Othello publicly slaps Desdemona in the face. In Act IV, ii, Othello directly confronts Desdemona with the accusation of adultery. He refuses to accept her denial, but, from the audience's point of view (the audience, that is, which has not already seen or read the play) the possibility exists up to that moment that Desdemona might convince Othello to the contrary. From this point on, there is no real possibility of Othello's turning back, though even in the death scent of Act V, ii, the audience still hopes that Desdemona may be able to say something that will clear her. In V, i, the attempt is made on Cassio's life, to which Othello was a prior party.

The Conclusion Or Denouement:

The falling action flows almost imperceptibly into the **denouement**, and it is almost arbitrary to say where one ends and the other begins. The killing of Desdemona is, in one sense, a final act of the tragedy, but the play is so constructed that a good deal of explanation is called for, particularly in regard to the unmasking of Iago. Emilia stumbles on the facts of Iago's intrigue. Othello, overcome with shock and remorse, kills himself.

Question: How does Shakespeare use poetry in *Othello?*

Answer: While the poetry of Shakespeare has general characteristics, each major work also reveals individual qualities. Modern criticism has emphasized the study of the predominant **imagery** of a play, the "image-clusters," the interrelationships of images. As one critic has put it, "profusion of images is so handled through a long play that it forms a systematic structure and is part of the plot." Dr. Robert Heilman has made a major study of this kind in *Magic in the Web: Action and Language in Othello.*

Different people are apt to favor different kinds of poetry. If by poetry we have in mind primarily rich and complex imagistic expression, we may be more impressed by the poetry of a *King Lear* or an *Anthony and Cleopatra*. But there is also a different way of looking at dramatic poetry; the poetical element may be used sparingly but with tremendous impact, because of careful spacing and timing. Othello presents a very special type of human intrigue, and use is made of a proportionally higher amount of direct prose (particularly in the Iago-Roderiga exchanges) than in the other great tragedies. But the overtly poetical, when it is employed, is dramatically most effective.

Othello himself moves against a background of the romantic and the mysterious. As Helen Gardner says, "Othello is like a hero of the ancient world in that he is not a man like us, but a man recognized as extraordinary. He seems born to do great deeds and live in legend." But it is in keeping with Oohello's frank and forthright personality, even with his background as a soldier, to speak in concrete and imagistic terms, though infrequently in **metaphor**. His long autobiographical account (I, iii) evokes a poetic atmosphere, but not one true **metaphor** can be found in it. Occasionally, under the stress of great emotion, Othello symbolizes his feelings by some great scene drawn from nature:

. . . O my soul's joy! If after every tempest come such calms, May the winds blow till they have waken'd death! And let the laboring bark climb hills of sea Olympus-high and duck again as low As hell's from heaven!

On another, but horrible, occasion, when he joins with Iago in taking the oath of revenge, his mind reverts to a similar sea image:

. . . Like to the Pontic sea Whose icy current and compulsive course Ne'er feels retiring ebb . . .

Othello's description of the heirloom handkerchief is poetic but not metaphorical-it is mysterious but factual:

The worms were hallow'd that did breed the silk; And it was dyed in mummy which the skillful Conserv'd of maidens' hearts.

It is in direct confrontation with Desdemona that Othello breaks into emotion-laden and telling metaphors:

Where either I must live, or bear no life; The fountain from the which my current runs, Or else dries up . . .

He uses concentrated and complex **imagery** symbolizing disgust, frustration, even love: "a cistern for foul toads / To knot and gender in!"

It is in the final scene that the sparingly used poetic **metaphor** comes to life with devastating power: "Put out the light, and then put out the light" and "When I have plucked thy rose, / I cannot give is vital growth again." The image of whiteness harrows Othello: "O ill-starr'd wench! / Pale as thy smock!" In reference to himself, he returns to his favorite sea images:

Here is my journey's end, here is my butt, And very sea-mark of my utmost sail.

Poetic **metaphor** is infrequently used in *Othello,* but, when used, it has maximum emotional effect.

Helen Gardner sums up the essence of Othello's poetic statement in these words: "Wonder is the note of Othello's greatest poetry, felt in the concreteness of its **imagery** and the firmness of its rhythms. Wonder sharpens our vision of things, so that we see them, not blurred by sentiment, or distorted by reflection, but in their own beautiful particularity."

Question: What main factors enter into a stage production of *Othello?*

Answer: An excellent study of the history of stage production of *Othello* is to be found in Marvin Rosenberg's *The Masks of Othello*. Such a history serves as a balance and corrective to the detailed analysis of the critic in the library. The reaction of an audience is apt to point out whether a given interpretation makes good sense or is "far out." This relationship, of course, also works the other way around. The analysis of the critic has often given the actor a valuable "tip" on how to proceed.

Historically the Shakespearean stage provided a certain intimacy between the actor and the audience that is missing today, except in so far as an effort is made to recapture the original conditions of Shakespeare's theater. Without going into its many technical details, we may say that the "projecting" stage (that is, a stage that jutted out in the midst of the audience - the audience surrounding it on three sides) could provide the actor, when the script required it, with a "man-to-man" approach to the audience. We do not normally use soliloquies in modern plays. But an Iago uses many of them, coming right into the midst of the audience, allowing them confidential glimpses into his sinister mind.

A basic reference work for understanding the original technical problems of producing a Shakespearean play is that of

John C. Adams, *The Globe Playhouse: Its Design and Equipment.*
Dr. Adams' model of the Globe playhouse is to be found in the
Folger Shakespeare Library, Washington, D. C. The stage contains
eight units: forestage, middle stage, inner stage, balcony stage,
two window stages, the tarras (when the curtains of the balcony
stage were drawn, a space of about three feet extended to the
balustrade facing the audience-used for battlements, city
walls, and so on), and the musician's gallery. Such a stage was
extremely fluid and versatile. Cecile de Banke in *Shakespearean
Stage Production: Then and Now* places the scene (I, ii) where
the Brabantio and Othello forces meet, on the forestage (the
projecting part of the total stage). "Scenes which are 'before' a
building but do not require the background" - if these are also
very important-are played on the forestage. This would be true
of the scene in which Othello demands the handkerchief from
Desdemona (III, iv), and of the scene where Othello listens to
the exchanges between Iago and Casio (IV, i). The Shakespeare
theater made plentiful use of "combined-unit settings." Thus the
great senate scene (I, iii) would make use of the middle stage
(the assembled senators) and of the forestage (including the
Iago-Roderigo passages). In V, ii, Othello retreats to the inner
stage to find a new sword. Artistically the great advantage of
these arrangements is that instant use can be made either of one
or of a variety of stage "spaces." Curtains could be used for the
middle stage, where supporting pillars were stationed, or for
the inner stage, which was part of the main building and flush
with it. The forestage was open and could not be curtained.

Though not making extensive use of stage settings, the
Shakespeare theater was a colorful place. Magnificent jeweled
costumes were worn by certain of the principal characters;
the physical plant itself was decorated in gilt and lavish color.
Darkness itself can, of course, be a color, and this plays an
important part in the production of *Othello.* As Rosenberg

states: "... *Othello* is dappled with the **imagery** of night scenes that complement the dark-light of the felt life. Torches bob on murky streets, in the shadow plots are made; Venetians brawl at night, on Cyprus soldiers carouse and islanders riot; and in a dim, candle-lit chamber, a woman is killed. ... At the Globe, of an afternoon, it took a word and a flicker of a torch or candle to make darkness of daylight in the minds of an audience...."

The theater made extensive use of musical effects. Martial music is not used in *Othello,* although there exists a background of war, because Shakespeare emphasizes the domestic aspect of the tragedy. But use is made of ceremonial trumpets, as on Othello's arrival in Cyprus (II, i) and on the Herald's reading of the proclamation (II, ii).

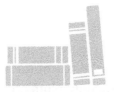

BIBLIOGRAPHY

ARTICLES

Bethell, S. L., "Shakespeare's **Imagery**: The Diabolic Images in *Othello*," Cambridge: Shakespeare Survey, 1952, pp. 62-80. Evaluates the meaning of these images in the play.

Elliott. G. R., "*Othello* as a Love-Tragedy," *The American Review*, VIII:3, January, 1937. An early example of the criticism that finds deficiency in the quality of his love as a tragic flaw in *Othello*.

Leavis, F. R., "Diabolic Intellect and the Noble Hero: A Note on *Othello*," *Scrutiny*, London, England, VI:3, December, 1937. This article also finds deficiency in *Othello*'s love.

Siegel, Paul N., "The Dammnation of *Othello*," *PMLA*, LXVIII:5 (December, 1953), pp. 1068-1078. Offers an interpretation of *Othello* in terms of religious tradition.

GENERAL: CLASSIC CRITICISM AND INTERPRETATIONS

Bradley, Andrew C., *Shakespearean Tragedy*, New York: Meridian Books, 1955. Paperback. Especially good on character analysis.

Campbell, Oscar James, *"King Lear,"* *The Living Shakespeare*, New York: The Macmillan Co., 1949.

Chambers, E. K., *Shakespeare: A Survey*, New York: Hill & Wang, 1958. Paperback.

Charlton, H. B., *Shakespearean Tragedy*, Cambridge: Cambridge University Press, 1961. Paperback. Good on the kind of world in which the action of Lear takes place.

Coleridge, Samuel Taylor, *Coleridge's Shakespearean Criticism*, Cambridge, 1930, and in many reprints. Valuable for the critical insights of a man who was himself a great poet.

Dowden, Edward, Shakespeare-A Critical Study of His Mind and Art, *New York: Harpers, 1918.*

Goddard, Harold C., *The Meaning of Shakespeare*, Chicago: University of Chicago Press, 1951.

Granville-Barker, Harley, *Prefaces to Shakespeare*, Princeton: Princeton University Press, 1946. The classic work on Shakespeare's stagecraft and on the plays in actual performance.

Hazlitt, William, *Characters of Shakespeare's Plays*, London, 1870, and often reprinted. Insights of one of the greatest Romantic critics.

Holznecht, Karl J., *The Backgrounds of Shakespeare's Plays*, New York: American Book Co., 1950.

Knight, G. Wilson, *The Wheel of Fire*, New York: Meridian Books, 1957. Paperbound. Intensely poetic and interesting reading of the play.

Kott, Jan, Shakespeare, *Our Contemporary*, Garden City, New York: Doubleday, 1964.

Lamb, Charles, "On the Tragedies of Shakespeare," in *The Works of Charles Lamb*, London, 1818, and in many reprints. Very influential criticism, originates idea that Lear is too big for any stage and is best appreciated when read.

Nicoll, Allardyce, *Studies in Shakespeare*, New York: Harcourt Brace, 1927.

Spencer, Theodore, *Shakespeare and the Nature of Man*, New York: The Macmillan Co., 1949.

Spurgeon, Caroline, *Shakespeare's **Imagery***, London: Cambridge University Press, 1935. Influential study of the **similes** and metaphors, and how they affect the meaning of the play.

Stampfer, J., "The Catharsis of *King Lear*," *Shakespeare Survey* 13, ed. Allardyce Nicoll, Cambridge: Cambridge University Press, 1960, pp. 1-10.

Swinburne, Algernon C., *Three Plays of Shakespeare*, London:

Harper, 1909. Especially interesting on religious attitudes in *Lear*, by an outstanding 19th century poet.

Tolstoy, Leo, *Tolstoy on Shakespeare*, New York: Funk & Wagnalls, 1906. An extremely hostile, provocative and wrongheaded personal interpretation by the great novelist. It should be read in connection with George Orwell. "Lear, Tolstoy and the Fool," in *Shooting an Elephant*, London: Secker & Warburg, 1950.

Traversi, D. A., *An Approach to Shakespeare*, New York: Doubleday Anchor, 1956. Paperback. One of the most stimulating modern interpretations.

Van Doren, Mark, *Shakespeare*, New York: Doubleday Anchor, 1953. Paperback. A sane, simple approach.

BACKGROUND OF IDEAS

Campbell, Lilly B., *Shakespeare's Tragic Heroes: Slaves of Passion*, New York: Barnes and Noble, 1959. Connects Othello with contemporary theories of the passions.

Grace, William J., *Approaching Shakespeare*, New York: Basic Books, 1964. A very helpful introduction to Shakespeare's methods of dramatic art and of poetry. Contains an analysis of *Othello*.

Haydn, Hiram, *The Counter-Renaissance*, New York: Charles Scribners, 1950. A thorough study of the intellectual background of the Renaissance period, with numerous references to Shakespeare. The index should be consulted on *Othello*.

McCollom, William, *Tragedy*, New York: Macmillan, 1957. Useful in considering the various problems that enter the art of tragedy.

Spencer, Hazelton, *The Art and Life of William Shakespeare*, New York: Harcourt, Brace, 1940. A superior "omnibus" book.

Spencer, Theodore, *Shakespeare and the Nature of Man*, New York, Macmillan, 1949. A most valuable book showing how Shakespeare views the nature of man in his plays with reference to the philosophical problems of the time. Stresses the concern with the problem of appearance versus reality, with emphasis on Iago.

Stewart, J. I. M., *Character and Motive in Shakespeare*, New York: Hafner Publishing Co., 1949. Offers revealing insights into the motivations of Shakespeare's characters.

Tillyard, E. M. W., *The Elizabethan World Picture*, London: Chatto and Windus, 1952. A basic introduction to the commonly held ideas and values of Shakespeare's time.

Van Doren, Mark, *Shakespeare*, New York: Doubleday, 1953. A very helpful background book.

MAJOR CRITICAL WORKS

Bradley, A. C., *Shakespearean Tragedy*, London: Macmillan, 1932. A major study of Shakespeare's tragedies, discussed previously.

Coe, C. Norton, *Demi-devils: The Character of Shakespeare's Villains*, New York: Bookman Associates, 1962. Contains an interesting analysis of Iago.

Coleridge, Samuel Taylor, "Notes on *Othello*," in *Thomas Middleton Raysor, Coleridge's Shakespearean Criticism*, Cambridge: Harvard University Press, 1930, Vol. I, pp. 44-54. Some of this material is contained in the D. N. Smith anthology listed below.

Elliott, G. R., *Flaming Minister*, Durham: Duke University Press, 1953. Offers very illuminating commentaries on specific passages of *Othello*.

Granville-Barker, Harley, *Prefaces to Shakespeare,* Princeton: Princeton University Press, 1947, Vol. I. It contains a running commentary on *Othello* (pp. 3-149) by this famous producer of Shakespearean plays.

Hazlitt, William, "Characters of Shakespeare's Plays," contained in D. Nichol Smith, *Shakespeare Criticism: A Selection* (see below).

Heilman, Robert B., *Magic in the Web: Action and Language in Othello*, Lexington: University of Kentucky Press, 1956. This is a major critical study of *Othello* as a whole. It has been discussed previously.

Rosenberg, Marvin, *The Masks of Othello*, Berkeley: University of California Press, 1961. This is a major study of the stage history of *Othello*. It also possesses many other insights. It has been discussed previously.

Siegel, Paul N., *Shakespearean Tragedy and the Elizabethan Compromise*, New York: New York University Press, 1957. Offers an interpretation of Othello in terms of religious tradition.

Sisson, C. J., *Shakespeare's Tragic Justice*, London, Methuen. 1961. This work explains how Othello comes to identify himself with divine justice. It illuminates a special area of the tragedy.

Stoll, E. E. *Art and Artifice in Shakespeare*, Cambridge: Cambridge University Press, 1933. The thesis of this book is that characters should be viewed in terms of the actual performance of the drama. Has interesting comments on Iago.

ANTHOLOGIES OF CRITICISM

Dean, Leonard, A *Casebook on Othello*, New York: Thomas Y. Crowell, 1961. A very useful collection of critical essays.

Smith, D. N. *Shakespeare Criticism: A Selection*, London: Oxford University Press, 1961. Often reprinted, this little book contains much of the older general criticism, with a number of references to *Othello*.

Ridler, Ann, *Shakespeare Criticism*, 1935-60, London: Oxford University Press, 1963. It contains Helen Gardner, "The Noble Moor," a *British Academy Lecture*, 1955. This essay stresses *Othello* as "heroic man."

STAGE PRODUCTION

Adams, John Cranford, *The Globe Playhouse: Its Design and Equipment*, Cambridge: Harvard University Press, 1942. This is a primary classic in the field of the technical aspects of the Elizabethan theater.

De Banke, Cecile, *Shakespearean Stage Production: Then and Now*, New York: McGraw-Hill, 1953. An informative book on the technical aspects of production.